CRUSHED BUT NOT DESTROYED

A Story of triumph in the face of great adversities

RICHARD KOJO ACHEAMPONG

FLYBOOKS
PUBLISHING

LONDON

First published in Great Britain in 2023
by FlyBooks Publishing
www.flybooks.co.uk

Published in the United Kingdom by FlyBooks Publishing,
London.

ISBN: 978-1-7395395-0-4

Printed in the United Kingdom by Degraf Digital.

DEDICATION

I dedicate this book to Mary Hentall, Margaret Dell, Diana Imelda Corbin, Mfom James, and all the medical staff who worked on Aspen and Beech wards at Barnet General Hospital London between the period September 1998 to March 1999.

CONTENTS

INTRODUCTION

We all have moments in our lives that define us. Events that make us who we are. My story is about these moments.

It is also about how we, as human beings, live within a paradox. How the world sees us and how we see ourselves differently. Our public face may smile and laugh. It may show pride or exude welcome, but in most cases, it will not reveal our scars.

Few of us truly understand the battles others have faced. So yes, my story is an opportunity to share my battles so that others understand them, the battle for my identity, sanity, and fundamental sense of being.

Yet this is not a story of despair.
It is one of hope.

I am Richard Kojo Acheampong, a man who triumphed despite innumerable odds. When people look at me, they see a broad grin and a smart suit. A lawyer qualified in two jurisdictions (England and Wales and Ghana), the owner of a multi-million-pound business, and a loving father and husband. A man who came to England from Ghana with nothing and made it work.

But beneath that public face are so many scars, physical and psychological. I could have given up on several occasions, and if not for the help of a few wonderful people, I may not have prevailed to tell my tale.

I will talk about all my scars in time, but one particular event underpins all the rest. My defining moment happened on North London street late at night in 1998. I was just 26 years old, full of ambition and ideas.

The speeding car that hit me came out of nowhere. I did not see it. Not until it was too late, anyway. Its impact flung me onto the pavement, and it did not stop.

As I lay there, barely conscious, blood haemorrhaging inside my leg, I did not yet fully understand that my injuries were severe and life-altering. My life, as I had known it, was over.

So, I am dedicating this book to the wounded people, the damaged people, and those who feel lost.

I was once one of you. In some ways, I still am.

Somehow, I managed to cling to everything I dreamed of and everything I believed in. It was not easy, but I did it. Then, piece by piece, I made a new life.

And if I can so, can you.

CHAPTER ONE

DETERMINED

My adult life has been based around London, one of the world's busiest, wealthiest, and most iconic cities, where almost anything is possible, good, or bad. My childhood, however, was spent somewhere quite different. I was born and raised in a small township called Nkonya Ntumda in the Volta region of Eastern Ghana.

Nkonya is a traditional area in Ghana, in which people identify as a tribe known as Guan Kponkpos. There are nine towns in the area, of which Ntumda is one. Each town had its own chief and sub-chiefs.

My village was home to around two thousand people and consisted of a main road lined by simple, one-storey buildings, mainly bungalows constructed from clay bricks, with two churches, the Roman Catholic church, and Evangelical Presbyterian church at the southern and northern edges of the town respectively.

Beyond the village limits lay great fields, an abundance of farms, and the stunning blue Omla mountains. It was (and is) a beautiful place, with clean, fresh air and a tangible closeness to nature. But it was also a very poor place.

My father had two wives, as is common in Ghana. I was my mother's fifth child of eight and my father's fifth child of fourteen. My father was a teacher and moved around depending on which postings he received. During my childhood, he spent most of his time in another village called Tepo with his family there, meaning I grew up with my maternal siblings, my mother, and my grandmother, in humble circumstances.

We lived in what was called a compound house. This consisted of a shared kitchen and eating area, surrounded by a collection of single rooms in which each family would sleep. My bed was a large mat on the floor, which I shared with my brothers.

Despite that, in some ways, it was a wonderful environment for a small child. The families would share food, and the children would play together, which created a lovely, communal atmosphere. But other aspects of our life were not quite as pleasant.

Our village had a pipe connected to a pumping machine to collect water. Often the machine would malfunction. There would be a wait for it to be repaired, during which we had to walk three kilometres to the river instead. Sometimes that machine was broken for six months at a time, and all the families of Ntumda would head out of town with buckets, pots, and kegs every morning. Walking to the river was easy but coming back, carrying heavy containers of water was hard work.

Even from an extremely young age, I was aware of our poverty. Not that I dwelled on it or allowed it to upset me, but I recognised it. It was not what I wanted my family to be associated with.

My mother, Grace Aboegey, was a trader and farmer, just like most people in the village, but it was difficult to make ends meet. She sold vegetables, corn, cassava, and other things which could be grown locally.

My oldest brother, William, whom my mother had when she was barely nineteen, was a brilliant child, and Mum invested everything she had in him. He went to one of the best schools, and the idea was that eventually, he would grow up, take up a profession and be able to support the family. As a youngster, I looked up to this tall, handsome, articulate teenager. All I wanted was to be like him.

My sister Mabel and I had to stay with my father for a few years in a place called Bethel. He had been posted there as the head teacher of a school. At the time, Mum was struggling to care for all of us alone. She visited occasionally and would stay for a month or two, before going to Ntumda. I enjoyed staying with him as he afforded me a great deal of freedom. When, on one of her visits, Mum found out I had been fishing at a place where the river Black Volta meets the White Volta, a strange place with two different colours of water flowing side by side, she exploded with rage. It was known to be a dangerous spot, and she did not like the teacher I had gone with. She could not believe my father had allowed me to go there.

After Mum found out about the fishing expedition, I soon found myself back in Nkonya Ntumda with her. Soon my father's placement in Bethel ended and he returned to Tepo, which was just two kilometres away. One day, shortly after returning from my stay with my father, I came home from school to find Mum with a very sombre expression on her face.

'Kojo,' she said. 'We have to leave our house.'

I was bewildered. It may not have been much, but it was our home. I had no desire to leave.

'Why?' I asked.

Mum would not tell me. She just kept repeating that we had to leave, and within a week, we packed up our things. Mum had managed to arrange some alternative accommodation for us. Sadly, it was not much of an alternative.

There was a dilapidated house just behind the one we had lived in, owned by my aunty. It was small and in poor condition and had been used previously as lodgings for labourers from nearby villages to work on my aunt's farm. By this point, it had lain empty for several years and had fallen into disrepair, but it seemed this was the best we could do.

When I saw the state of our new home, I vehemently expressed my disagreement with the setting. I was old enough at this point to insist on something if I thought it necessary.

'No, I told mum'. 'We cannot go there!'

Slowly, the truth emerged. William, who by then was in his early twenties, had developed mental health problems. His behaviour became strange. He stopped washing and started walking around, talking to himself loudly, sometimes pushing people for no reason. He even undressed or went to the toilet in the middle of the street on one occasion. He had become a total nuisance.

Views of mental illness and, to some degree, illness, in general, were very much grounded in superstition in rural Ghana in those days. The notion was that if you were afflicted by poor health in this way, there had to be payback at work, that God was punishing you for some terrible sin you or your family had committed. People speculated that William was on drugs or even possessed by evil spirits. Because of this, he became a pariah in the village and the elders of the town wanted him kept indoors or removed from the town. Willian was sometimes chained down like a criminal to prevent him from roaming the town. Seeing my idol chained down was heartbreaking. I will often cry when I saw William chained down or when Mum was in distress. The owners of our first house, like most people in Ntumda, wanted nothing to do with William, so we had effectively been evicted. There was nothing we could do about it.

The situation had a terrible effect on our family in two ways. Firstly, our living conditions worsened. Our new house was hardly fit for purpose, tiny and windowless.

Secondly, my mother's dreams, previously centred around her belief that William would one day raise us out of poverty, were dashed. Not only would he not do that, but he had become an additional burden for the family, incapable of work. Villagers taunted us so harshly that going to certain areas or approaching certain people became difficult. It was a crushing blow for her.

It was a difficult thing for my family to come to terms with. Mum was very preoccupied with William's condition and often accompanied him to doctors' appointments and stayed in mental hospitals. The rest of us were left in the care of our grandmother. For me, I was faced with the reality that my role model, my inspirational older brother who I wanted to emulate, had changed so much. It was distressing, and I went through a period of inner conflict about it. After a while, I came to a realisation.

'Richard,' I said to myself one day. 'It is your turn now. You must step into William's shoes. You are the one who will lift this family up.'

I felt the words like fire inside me..

I was eleven years old.

As a result of William's illness, I turned to my father as a role model.

I began to make a point of walking the two kilometres to Tepo every now and then to visit my father and my siblings. Mum did not like this, but I kept at it, as I felt it was crucial to remain connected to both sides of the family. In time, she learned to accept it, so I became a bridge between the two houses, which I have maintained throughout my life.

As a backdrop to all of this, there was a brutal famine in Ghana during this period. There had been little meaningful rain for two years, and wildfires raged across the countryside. The resulting major crop losses affected everyone. What little food remained available skyrocketed in price. The situation was bad enough that a new phrase entered the Ghanaian lexicon, 'Rawlings chain,' which referred to the deep gorges formed around people's necks when they become emaciated, and their collar bones protruded.

Eventually, as this traumatic spell played itself out, we lost William. It was unlikely he died a natural death. Not as far as we knew, at least. He just disappeared. Of course, it was possible that as his condition worsened, he had wandered off into the wilderness and suffered an accident, but there were many rumours. We suspected, as did many people, that he may have been killed by some of the townsfolks. We never found his body. I have never stopped grieving his loss.

I was still a young boy and seeking my own way. I lived with these troubles in my hometown and family the way children do. None of us chooses the circumstances into which we are born; we just get on with life. But I think these events deepened my determination. A steely resolve grew inside me. Life had to be better.

A man in the village known as Nana Alafia ran a kind of herbal medicine business. His products were popular in

Ghana, and he made good money compared to other local people. He owned a classic Mercedes car and lived in the grandest house in Nkonya Ntumda. One day, I accompanied my mother there to buy some of his goods and was struck by the incredible difference between his living conditions and ours.

'Mum,' I asked, 'Why does Nana Alafia live in such a wonderful house while we have nothing?'

Mum turned to me. Perhaps she had been waiting for this opportunity. 'Kojo, she said, 'Listen, work hard, make me proud, and do your very best. And one day, you can live like Nana Alafia.'

There was a strange light in her eyes as she spoke, and just for a moment, the village around us seemed to fall silent. That was when I knew her dreams of a better future now rested with me.

A few days later, Mum returned home from her farm. We had a row with my cousin and her children about the house we were living in. It got quite heated. Everyone was upset.

'Mama,' I told her once things had simmered down, I will build a house for you one day.'

Just saying those words out loud seemed to give them weight. I had made a promise to her and to myself. I immediately began working as hard as I could. Soon, I was just ahead of my sister in school. We both attended primary school in the village. That conversation with my mother drove me on. Soon I was first in all subjects. I read in my spare time and learned to speak English. As I neared the end of my time at primary school, they made me a prefect. I was not a genius, and I knew that, but I was the most determined.

Determination, I would soon discover, could make all the difference.

CHAPTER TWO

A RISING STAR

At ten years old, I moved from my local primary school in Nkonya Ntumda to the middle school nearby. It is important to note that in Ghana, this was not a compulsory step. Many children finished with formal education altogether after primary school and began work, usually on farms. Of course, my ambitions were greater than that.

Ghanaian primary education at the time was run by the government, independent, religious, or private organisations. In my village, there were two primary schools, the Evangelical Presbyterian (EP) primary and the Roman Catholic primary (RC), and pupils from RC and EP progressed to the Local Authority middle school (LA).

The story was that the RC pupils were academically better than the EP pupils because they had always had better facilities and better teachers.

Before I entered LA middle school at Ntumda, no EP pupil had ever come first in the terminal exams. I was determined to change this narrative, and I did so in my first year at the middle school.

One of my teachers, Mr Nyavo at the LA middle school, identified with me, as he was a member of the EP church which ran the EP primary school. When I broke the long-standing record held by pupils from RC primary, he said 'Richard, you will be my first graduate.' I laughed. Somehow that prophesy, if it was one, has been fulfilled.

Perhaps it was because of his special interest and encouragement, married with my own clear focus, that I soon became the number-one achieving pupil in my year group.

At the age of thirteen, I moved on to secondary school. The school I attended had boarding facilities, but I was a day student, meaning I had to walk about two kilometres there and back daily for the first three years. It also required a uniform.

I moved to the boarding house in my fourth year and on my first day, I met the dormitory prefect, Gustav. He took an immediate liking to me and took me under his wing.

'Richard,' Gustav said to me. 'You are a brilliant boy. But there's not much time in this world. You must make every second count.'

Gustav and I would wake up every morning at 4 a.m. to go and study. There was a roster of chores students were directed to undertake, so after an hour of hitting the books, we would complete our housework before the school bell rang at 6 a.m. It was a demanding regime, but one I actually enjoyed.

One of my aunties bought me a shirt, which turned out to be a woman's blouse. She made some adjustments with a needle and thread, but it was still visibly different from the shirts of the other pupils. Nonetheless, I remained steadfast, and that blouse was my school shirt for the first two years there.

Shoes were a constant bother, too, as they tended to wear out. Sometimes I even borrowed shoes from my sisters that I could wear to save on cost.

It was a time of hard work in general, but happy hard work. I had a sense of destiny that fuelled everything I did. I collaborated with one of my older cousins, Emmanuel Danso, during the school holidays to help him on his farm. We got on very well, and he loved me like a little brother.

As a reward for my efforts, Emmanuel gave me a piece of virgin land I could cultivate for myself, which I found incredibly exciting.

The land amounted to about three acres on the mountainside but was heavily populated by trees. Before I could cultivate anything, I would need to clear some space. So, for help, I sought out my father.

'Papa,' I said, 'I need a little money'. I have to rent a chainsaw, to remove the trees from my land'. 'Really' he asked.

My father could see that I was serious and lent me the money. As soon as I received the money I needed, I got to work immediately with Mum helping me every step of the way.

My main crop was cocoyam (also known as mankeni), a root vegetable that forms an important part of the diet of many Ghanaians. Both the leaves and the roots can be eaten, making it a popular staple. I also grew plantain, which some Europeans call 'cooking bananas'. Again, these are a common part of everyday, West African cuisine.

Before long, my farm was up and running. As I poured my energies into it, it was as if there was magic at work, it flourished magnificently.

The land must have been very fertile. The cocoyam stalks became very big and tall. Over time, my farm became an attraction. From the village, if you looked up to the mountain, you could see the farm. When visitors came close to the farm, they were amazed by the huge, bright yellow cocoyam flowers. Yes, the cocoyam plants flowered which does not happen on many farms! People would point and remark on it.

At a young age, my success in farming proved to me that hard work could pay off, and it proved financially lucrative too. I found myself in the fortunate position of continuing my studies and working towards a future while making a good living in the present. I could also give my mother money to contribute towards the household expenses.

My academic life was also progressing well. While coming to the end of my Ordinary level (GCSC) education, I entered an essay competition organised by the Royal Commonwealth Society. The topic was 'How sports can unite people,' and as ever, I put my heart and soul into my work.

At eighteen, I finished the Ordinary level phase of my secondary school and moved on to Okuapeman School, one of the finest A-level schools in another part of the country. My new place of learning was a six-hour bus journey from Nkonya-Ntumda, which meant staying away from home.

I settled in at Okuapeman very well and became known as the pupil who was good with words. I enjoyed developing my vocabulary and language skills and was not afraid to use phrases I had learned in books in my speech.

Some of the children at the school had well-off parents, and at first, that bothered me a little. I wondered how I could fit in with these children, but I became great friends with a boy called Isaac Odonkor, who helped me out by letting me borrow clothes and shoes when mine were no longer presentable.

Through the kindness of Isaac and my own pride, I kept my head and did not allow my background to hold me back. I competed with my schoolmates as an equal and was top of the class in Geography.

The crowning achievement of my time at Okuapeman School came when the result of the essay competition I had entered while at Nkonya Secondary was announced.

One day, I received an unexpected message telling me to report to the assistant headteacher's office. He was known as 'CJ' by the students, and if you were summoned to see him, it was usually serious. As I walked there, my head was spinning with questions. What had I done wrong? Why on earth would CJ ask me to come to his office?

When I arrived, however, some visitors were waiting to speak to me. They had come to deliver a letter to me from the Royal Commonwealth Society, which CJ read aloud.

My essay won first prize for the whole of West Africa in my category. It was a tremendous honour, and I was invited to attend the presentation ceremony in Accra, Ghana's capital city.

Publicity followed, with my name in the newspapers, and the whole sequence of events was like a fantastic dream. I was taken to Accra and stayed in a hotel for the first time in my life.

At the ceremony itself, there was a great deal of talk about me, and I was invited to say a few words. It was a wonderful experience, which proved to me how much this could mean. My hard work and commitment to my education could reap exciting rewards and expand the horizons of my life beyond anything I could have imagined.

On my return to Okuapeman School, it was evident how much the school had revelled in my success. The news had spread throughout the school and announcements on school and house notice boards were on full display. My housemaster (Mr Teyegaga) made much noise about the news at the Sunday house assembly. As I walked the corridors again, it was as if I had become a celebrity.

'Is it you?' Other students would ask. 'Are you Richard Acheampong, the boy who won the award?'

Everybody wanted to speak to me and offer their congratulations. My family, of course, were very proud too.

I finished my A levels, and it was obvious that a course of study at university lay in my future. However, it was not possible to begin that straight away. First, I had to earn some money.

I got a job working for the Ghana Statistical Service in Accra and was immediately put on a project which involved travelling around the country and conducting surveys. The data we gathered was mostly concerned with the health and living standards of people in Ghana and was used by the United Nations and the Ghanaian government to inform the basis of their policymaking.

While doing this job, I was sent to a particular rural village in the north of the country, where there was an issue regarding the local chieftains. This sounds strange to outsiders, but the traditional way of life still has a significant hold over people in Ghana. Chiefs are treated like gods, and there are often conflicts and even deaths if disputes arose concerning chieftaincy matters.

As a result, the situation we were sent into was potentially volatile, and almost as soon as we arrived in the village, we were surrounded by locals. It seemed the faction we met supported one chief, but one of my colleagues, a Ghanaian who had been abroad for a long time and misunderstood the local dynamics, inadvertently mentioned the name of a rival chief. Immediately that provoked a hostile reaction, and we were told in no uncertain terms that we needed permission to remain on the chief's territory. Soon we were being dragged off to meet him, with the implicit understanding that if the chief did not give us his blessing, we were in big trouble.

Our group was of mixed nationality, and some of my colleagues were frightened out of their minds. I was the only one who had grown up in a rural Ghanaian village and I felt I understood the scenario well.

We were taken through a series of gates and outbuildings into the palace. The chief sat before us in the middle of the floor on a cowskin. He wore a smock and an elaborate piece of headgear adorned with beads and cowries.

The chief beckoned us forwards, and I did my best to communicate with him. This was not straightforward, as there are many different dialects in Ghana, but of all of us present, I had the best chance.

I had not been talking long when the chief smiled broadly. He asked one of his elders to bring me a calabash (a gourd) containing a type of porridge, another Ghanaian tradition.

When it was brought to me, I took it with both hands and ate it as enthusiastically as I could. Apparently, this was a way of welcoming a stranger and testing whether he or she accepts the values and culture of his host. The chief smiled and asked me to come and sit with him on the cowskin.

I could tell as I walked forward that the other people in the room were shocked. The cowskin held special significance and was almost considered a sacred part of the room. For anyone to sit there other than the chief was a huge honour.

It emerged that the chief could speak English, and we began to converse. I explained to him what our work involved, and he seemed genuinely interested.

Once I had finished, he passed my information on to some of his elders, who were then tasked with disseminating it to the people.

As a result, we could stay in the area for five days to complete our survey, enjoying the hospitality of the chief; he had three wives, who took turns cooking three meals a day for us, and we stayed in the lodgings he arranged.

When our work was finished, the chief summoned us again to the palace. As usual, he seemed extremely pleased to see me, and as he bade me goodbye, he made me a gift of ten tubers of yam and three guinea fowls, and then he leaned a little closer.

'My daughters,' he said to me knowingly.

As might be expected of a man with three wives, he had a huge number of children.

'You can take any of them,' he went on, 'And if you want, you can marry them.'

To begin with, I thought it was a joke. One of his daughters, who was about fifteen or sixteen and very adorable, stood nearby, so I thought I would play along.

'This is the one I want,' I said, pointing.

The chief's face became solemn. 'Then you have my blessing,' he said.

The girl nodded demurely, and it soon became apparent that this was entirely serious. She was prepared to leave the village with me, so I had to think of something.

'Sir' I said, 'Your offer is very kind, but we are still on the road and will be travelling for some time. It is not appropriate for me to take your daughter now.'

He accepted the news stoically, and we left shortly afterwards. As we made our way along the bumpy road in our Land Rover, I could not help but reflect on what had just happened. If I wanted to, I could have been returning to Accra as a married man. My colleagues were all surprised at how events had unfolded.

'There is something different about you, Richard.' One of them said to me.

A short while after that assignment, I returned to Nkonya Ntumda to visit my mother. She was very impressed when I told her about the chief.

'Kojo,' she told me, 'You see, you have a wonderful effect on people. The chief must have believed you are a very good person to want to give you his daughter.'

It seemed there was something about me that had come from my upbringing perhaps, which enabled me to build positive relationships with other people. I always seemed to be welcomed wherever I went.

That was a good thing because, in my mind, I had already formed aspirations to try my luck far away. My intention remained to improve my family's conditions beyond their wildest dreams, and it felt like nothing could stop me.

In 1996, I finally started university, studying Political Science at the University of Ghana in Accra. I settled in well, and along with my studies, I made conscious efforts to remain active.

All my life to this point, I had been very fit due to all my work on farms. I knew that at university, with all the desk work, I would lead a more sedentary life, so I made it a habit to go running for 5km or so at least three mornings a week. The university grounds were beautiful, and I enjoyed the ritual of the exercise and the focus it gave me. Although fitness had never been my primary interest, I was an extremely healthy youth with a broad chest and a narrow waist. When you're young, you feel invincible, and I had energy to burn.

Soon, however, my first year was disrupted by a series of strikes by university staff. During one of the down periods, I spoke to one of my cousins.

'I really want to go abroad,' I told her. To this point in my life, I had never left Ghana.

'Well, maybe you should,' she replied.

'But I don't have money,' I said.

We talked for a while and came up with a money-making scheme involving tomato farming. We knew they grew very well in the Barekesi district, in the Ashanti region of Ghana, so we visited a chief in a village called Amanfrom. I leased a piece of land averaging about five acres to cultivate tomatoes.

What resulted was a profitable little business in which I harvested thirty boxes of tomatoes every seven days for two months from Amanfrom. Before very long, I had made enough money to buy a plane ticket and pay for a hotel.

Over the years, I had been very aware of Ghanaians who had travelled to England, found work of some kind, and returned home with lots of money in their pockets. That was very attractive to me, but more than anything, I was drawn to dreams of London.

I had read about the London School of Economics (LSE), widely regarded as one of the world's top universities. The father of a friend of mine had studied there, and I nursed the ambition to do the same. How exciting that would be, for a boy from Nkonya Ntumda to further his education at such a prestigious institution. Perhaps if I went to London, I could speak to someone about the possibility or at least visit the campus.

So, I acquired a visa through the British Universities North American Club (BUNAC) and booked my flight for June 1998. An old acquaintance of mine called Collins was already there, staying in a house with other people from my community, in Stanmore, North West London. I had been in touch with him through his father and told him I was coming.

When the day came to travel, the journey was an experience; boarding the plane, eating the meal served onboard, and seeing London below us as we descended toward Heathrow. It was all unbelievably exciting for me.

This, I was certain was the start of something special.

CHAPTER THREE

LONDON

After arriving in London, BUNAC gave us a kind of tour for a week, which blew my mind. Even mundane things like travelling on the underground were so novel and exhilarating for me. I had never been on an escalator before, and I found the experience thrilling and sometimes frightening. It was as if I was in a giant theme park, and I could not help but be impressed by my new surroundings.

BUNAC then organised us to work as strawberry pickers at a farm near Rochester in Kent, which was easy for me because it was the kind of work, I had been doing throughout my childhood back home. On my first day, I picked thirty trays. The farmer, a pleasant man called Jimmy, was blown away.

'How the hell did you do that?' he asked. 'The next best person today picked twelve!'

'Man, don't you know where I come from?' I laughed.

The following morning, my co-workers were still aching and bent over from the previous day's work. On the other hand, I was completely fine and could start where I had left off.

After a week in Rochester, we returned to London, and I called Collins from the train station. He told me to come up to Edgware tube station and that he would meet me there.

Although I had enjoyed my experiences in England up to this point, it was still lovely to see a familiar face. We embraced. Collins expressed how proud of me he was that I had made it to university and acquired a visa to visit England. He asked if I was hungry and took me to a nearby KFC. At last, I got to try the famous KFC I had heard so much about. It made me so happy!

We then went to the house where he was staying, which was fully occupied by people from Ntumda and Tepo. Everyone was so delighted to see me. Amazingly, Henry, from my hometown also lived in the house. How refreshing it was, to fly halfway around the world and still meet someone from Nkonya Ntumda.

It was a happy little time, everyone was friendly and supportive, and we shared food. Collins was mostly working on Saturday and Sunday nights. When he was not there, I slept in his room. The rest of the time, I made do with the sofa in the lounge.

After a week or so, Henry found me some work. I cleaned a betting shop in the early morning, then went to a car dealership in Kingsbury to wash cars before finally going to the Royal National Orthopaedic Hospital in Stanmore for more cleaning work. This last job was an interesting one, in which my duties included cleaning the prosthetics unit, where amputees were fitted with artificial body parts. It was strange, and a little eerie, to work amongst all the legs, arms, hands, and feet waiting for their new owners. I used to talk about the wonderful prosthetic designs with my co-workers Eric and Agyei.

Overall, my workload was substantial and quite tiring. But I was happy to do it, as it was not in my nature to live on other people's money.

Despite that, or maybe because of it, I was a little surprised when Collins approached Henry with the suggestion that if I was staying there in the house, I should pay rent. I had been there two weeks by that time. Henry was not happy with this suggestion, was even a little offended by it, and it turned into a heated argument.

From my side, I was unsure why Collins took this attitude. I was not occupying a room, and my stay was only temporary. It was not very Ghanaian of him to be so unwelcoming.

The argument was so bad that it almost turned physical. In the aftermath, Collins could not put it behind him and decided to leave the house. Soon, he found alternative accommodation for us and suggested I move with him, and we would share the rent. My part came to two hundred and eighty Pounds (£280) a month, which on my meagre cleaner's earnings proved a struggle. I was only earning around six hundred and fifty Pounds (£650) for the three jobs I was doing.

Henry heard about this, took me to one side, and told me he did not want me to leave.

'It is not right, Richard,' he said. I will not allow you to go. You cannot afford it, and you are only here, in England, for eight weeks, anyway.'

So, I spoke to Collins and told him I would stay in the house with Henry. He was not happy with my decision.

'You have made your choice and that is it for us. If anything happens to you, I do not want to know.' Collins said.

And with that, he took his things and left. I sometimes found those words echoing around my mind. 'If anything happens to you…'

They would soon take on a very profound meaning.

At this stage, I had two and a half weeks remaining of my stay in England. My final year at university was due to begin in late September, and although I was enjoying my London, I was also eager to get back. I wanted to finish my degree, achieve a good result, and take that forward into a career or continue at LSE. That drive and ambition I had possessed since early childhood still burned inside me.

On the night of 3rd September 1998, I finished my shift at the hospital at 9 p.m. I was weary and looking forward to getting back to the house for food and sleep. Even though it was still autumn in England, I found the evenings cold and pulled my collars around my neck as I walked out of the hospital building. It was a typical night-time scene – a few people on the pavements, streetlights glowing orange, and the thick smell of petrol in the air.

The bus stop I needed for my ride home was across the street, and a bus had just pulled in. I looked both ways and saw that the road was clear in both directions, although on one side, my sight line was impaired by the crest of a hill. I stepped off the curb.

And that was the last thing I did before my life changed forever.

I was maybe halfway across the street when suddenly, the world span violently around me. I found myself lying across the street, surrounded by people previously waiting at the bus stop.

'Oh, my god! Are you all right; are you all right?' Someone asked.

I found it difficult to understand what was going on. Steadily, it became clear that I had been struck by a speeding car which I had neither seen nor heard. The car had not stopped, it sent me flying, and then disappeared into the night.

That is something I have often thought about in the years since. Two people were directly involved in the accident that night, a victim, and a perpetrator. I am not suggesting it was deliberate, but one person committed the act, and thc other suffered it. The intention is unimportant.

Yet while I have never been able to forget what happened and am reminded of it every second of every day, for the hit-and-run driver, it was fleeting and brief. They mowed me down in a split second and were gone.

For me, a lifetime. For them, the blink of an eye.

The only thing that could be described as lucky that night was that the accident happened so close to a hospital. Many bystanders who stood over me were nurses or other hospital staff who had just finished their shifts. As I looked up at them, bewildered, trying to understand what had happened, I was aware that my mouth felt very dry.

Suddenly a wave of agony swept through my body, and I screamed into the night for water.

'No, you can't drink water now.' A kind voice said.

I tried to sit up, but people were holding me down. I felt pressure in my legs and realised they were swelling inside my trousers. I tried to move my feet.

'Stay still, stay still,' another voice said.

The ambulance arrived extremely quickly, and before I could make sense of the situation, I was loaded onto a stretcher and wheeled away.

The first phase of my new life was about to begin.

CHAPTER FOUR

LOSING FAITH

My colleague and friend, Eric accompanied me in the ambulance. He sat with me and did his best to comfort me.

'Richard, don't worry, 'You'll be fine. It will all be OK' he said.

His presence helped to settle my mind, and by the time we arrived at Barnet General Hospital, I had recovered my senses well enough to give the names of my next of kin and other personal details. They informed me that I was badly hurt and would be taken into surgery for an operation. I had figured out as much myself but had no idea of any details.

The last thing I remember was being told that they had to cut off my trousers. The swelling in my legs was too acute for them to be removed normally. After that, the anaesthesia kicked in, and I drifted into unconsciousness.

I woke up to find myself in a hospital bed in a typical hospital room. Funnily enough, the first thing I saw clearly was a clock mounted on the wall opposite. It was 6 p.m. on 4th September 1998. That meant I had been unconscious for about sixteen hours.

My head was heavy, and I was aware of several tubes attached to my body. I could feel that my face was very puffy. Eric stood nearby, with Henry, my housemate from Stanmore.

There were two nurses in the room, one of whom, it seemed, was Ghanaian. She introduced herself as Bertha and stood over me.

Richard, you will be fine, she said.

They were the first words I had heard for such a long time.

'Why can't I move?' I croaked.

'You are in the hospital,' she explained. 'You can't move now. Just rest, and you will get better.'

Hours slipped by, and the following morning, I was told I would be moved. They wheeled my bed out of the emergency room and into Aspen ward, a surgical ward. Bertha insisted on staying with me and was transferred to Aspen ward for the day.

The ward was a large, open-plan room with a mixture of male and female patients. Again, time just seemed to drift. My body had been through a massive trauma, and even staying awake required a lot of energy. During my periods of lucidity, all I thought of was when could I go home. I wanted to return to Ghana to begin my final year and resume my studies. The fact that I was deemed well enough to transfer to the ward was a good sign, I thought. Surely, I knew my recovery was underway, and it would be just a matter of time before my injuries healed.

On the 6th of September, three days after my accident, I was visited by a doctor.

'When am I going to be discharged?' I asked him.

'Hmm?' He seemed a little thrown by the question.

'My university term starts in two weeks. I need to get back to Ghana.'

'Ah,' he said. 'Look, don't worry about that. We will look after you.'

He could see that I was confused. 'Let me tell you what has happened.' He paused. 'You have had a very terrible accident. There was a lot of damage. Some of your arteries were torn. You have had surgery and you are in recovery.'

I was not told at the time, but the truth was even more severe than the kind doctor presented it. I was later informed that my injuries were so bad that there had been crisis talks in the operating theatre. Two surgeons, Mr Loh, and Mr Bird had convened a very serious debate, during which Mr Bird had advocated that my right leg be amputated below the knee. He felt my injuries were too grave and there was no hope of recovery. Mr Loh, thankfully, had taken the view that something had to be tried; I was a young man with my whole life ahead of me, and losing a leg at twenty-six should only be a last resort.

Mr Loh had won the argument, and as a result, an attempt had been made to reconnect my horrifically damaged arteries. However, the procedure was extremely delicate, as my arteries were unusually small, which triggered a further discussion about whether to continue my treatment in England or fly me to Germany, where there was a specialist with expertise in such cases. Regardless, without Mr Loh's intervention, I would have woken up on 4th September 1998 with only one leg.

At this stage, the doctor was circumspect regarding the extent of my injuries, not wanting to worry me unduly and put me in a negative mental state. I guess this was his way of managing my emotion and apprehension. However, after reassuring me, he asked if I would like to see my leg.

'See it?'

'OK, Richard. We are going to remove the dressing and replace it. If you want, you can look.'

I agreed, with some apprehension. I did not know what to expect, but the doctor's cautious tone rang alarm bells in my head. I knew that if my injuries were inconsequential, there would have been no need for such a measured approach. They helped me sit up gently, and I was about to find out exactly why.

The doctor pulled back my bedsheets and started removing the dressings from around my leg. To begin with, it was a strange experience, as they were pumping me so full of drugs that there was no pain. I felt little tugs and pulls of pressure, but the dressings could almost have been attached to somebody else.

I looked away briefly as he pulled the last bandages off, then turned my head back. Immediately panic surged through my body. I felt a little sick. What I saw was worse than I could possibly have imagined. Without question, it was the worst injury I had ever seen.

My leg was effectively split open, with skin and muscle tissue hanging grotesquely from the clearly visible bone. It did not look like a human leg, just mangled flesh.

'You are not going back to university,' was the thought which passed through my mind. 'This will not heal in two weeks.'

Once I recovered from the shock, I offered an internal prayer. Throughout my life, I have always been a Christian, and faith is important to me. I was young and a good person with the hope of providing for my needy family. God would look after me, I was sure of it. I beseeched Him for help.

Later, Mr Loh came to visit me. He told me that, the next day, I would be undergoing surgery again, this time to have pins put in my leg. These would effectively hold the broken bones together, in the hope that they would heal.

As I recovered from this second surgery, I was cared for by a student nurse called Mfon James. She came with another nurse, Alice. Their faces and kindness did wonders for my mood. Mfon, in particular, took a special interest in me, and I began to look forward to her appearances.

'Oh, you must be Richard!' they said. 'We have heard about your accident. You have our sympathies. We will look after you.' They were such lovely company, and that was something I really needed. When you are at your most vulnerable, you really do learn the power of love.

Like the first time, a couple of days passed before I could see the leg. It looked better with the pins, more like an actual leg, and hope spiked inside me. Maybe this would all work out in the end.

But over the next few days or so, I realised that my right foot was becoming cold, and my toes were not moving correctly. Mr Loh asked the nurses to keep an eye on it and use extra blankets if necessary. Within another week, the foot began to swell, and I became fearful. It was not getting better. If anything, it seemed to be getting worse.

Mr Loh came back and spoke to me very quietly. 'Richard,' he said. 'You have to understand that you have had a terrible accident. Your blood supply system is compromised now, and there is not enough blood and oxygen reaching your foot. We will do everything we possibly can to save your leg, but we don't know how things will go.'

A lump rose in my throat. Those are not easy words to hear.

It was agreed that they would try a risky procedure involving injections into my spine, which could potentially enlarge my arteries. If it went wrong, there was a danger I would be paralysed. They attempted this twice over the next few weeks, with waiting periods to check for improvement. Sadly, the foot kept swelling, and my toes were turning black. They had gangrened.

They then grafted some skin from my thigh onto the wound to help it heal properly. I was encouraged to do little exercises with the leg to get the blood flowing. The hospital staff told me to eat as much as possible to assist in my recovery, which was hard for me as I found English food difficult to eat. Every day they brought me bread for breakfast, shepherd's pie or fish and chips for dinner, cakes, and salads. It was alien to me, but I did my best to force it down.

I had been in the hospital for about a month when Mr Loh came to see me again. He told me I would not see him for a short while as he was going on holiday, and I was to be transferred to another ward called Beech Ward. Again, I was very lucky that Mfon and Alice followed me there. They really did their best to make me feel positive.

After a couple of days in Beech ward, things took a turn for the worse. The swelling in my foot popped, and black pus began to ooze out. I was administered morphine because it was so excruciatingly painful.

Before long, Mr Loh appeared and spoke to me in my drugged state.

'Don't worry, Richard,' he said. 'I've come back to look after you. I have cancelled my holiday.'

At that moment, I felt like I was in the presence of Jesus Christ himself. 'The gangrene is moving too fast. We've got to stop it, or it can kill you. We need to make an incision under your foot to stop the gangrene.'

At that point, the penny dropped. I was not getting out of the hospital in one piece.

As if to confirm, the surgeon continued. 'We need to face reality here, Richard. We may need to amputate.'

My heart sank.

CHAPTER FIVE

A PART OF ME

Mr Loh prescribed me regular morphine, which did incredible things for my pain. I quickly became quite dependent on it, and a routine was established in which I received a dose every four hours.

The drug not only eased the physical distress caused by my injuries but also soothed me emotionally. When it kicked in, I felt at peace, but when its effects subsided, my mind burned with questions, anxieties, and pain.

How could this be happening? What had I done to deserve this?

Still, somewhere inside me, there flickered a flame of hope. I prayed and prayed, desperate for a miracle. I had been good all my life. I had worked hard and tried to honour my mother and father. I believed, with all my heart, God was capable of anything. Surely, he would not allow something so terrible to befall me.

I tried to mobilise my legs whenever possible to get the blood flowing.

By this point, my forefoot had turned black as the effects of the gangrene impacted areas adjacent to it. I was taken back to the operating theatre, and in the first instance, an incision was made to separate the gangrenous area from the rest of me, thus preventing the spread. Afterwards, as I recovered from yet another surgery, Mr Loh visited again.

'Richard', He said. I could tell by his demeanour that the news was not good. 'You were supposed to be in the theatre for thirty minutes today, but it took us nearly two hours. We found something bad. The skin around that part of your foot is dead. We removed it. I'm sorry. We have done everything we could, but we need to remove more. Not just skin, but other tissue, too. We are going to have to take off your forefoot.'

I am not proud to admit this, but as Mr Loh spoke those words, I lost faith in God. All my life, I had been a staunch believer in God. No more. Not as I lay on a hospital bed knowing something so important could be taken from me and God would not intervene despite all the prayers I said. A finger or even a part of an arm would be one thing. But a foot? How would I stand, walk, or run? It seemed unthinkable that this could really be happening.

Mr Loh tried to reassure me. He told me about prosthetics that would help me to be as mobile as possible. But I was overcome with desperation and despair. His words did not improve my state of mind.

From then on, and for quite a while, I stopped praying. What was the point? What was the point of anything anymore?

I felt I had let my family down. My mother knew I was in the hospital and had suffered an accident, but not the severity of it. How could I now tell her this?

All the dreams I had of providing for my parents and siblings seemed unachievable. Before, I had believed in them through the sheer invincibility of youth, but now my invincibility was gone. Soon I would just be a youth with one foot, an invalid. It was the darkest time of my life.

A date was set for 29th October, meaning there would be some wait until the operation would take place. It was such an incredibly difficult time, just lying there, helpless, knowing that this awful moment was coming.

To compound my misery, by this point, most of my regular visitors had disappeared. Eric, who was my regular visitor, had gone back to university. The visits from the Ghanaian community and colleagues, who had been present at the beginning reduced. Some had brought Ghanaian food in for me to eat – chicken stew or kenkey (a kind of dumpling made from corn), which was a great comfort to me. I still struggled so much with English food. But then, as perhaps is natural, when the situation extended itself and required a greater commitment of time, they all started drifting away, which was difficult for me to accept.

Once my fate had been confirmed, and I was waiting for the amputation to happen, I entered a state of enormous emotional and psychological vulnerability. That was when I most needed support. Not at the beginning when there was still so much light and hope. How on earth was I going to cope?

To make matters even worse, once I received a date for the operation, I called all of the people I knew and considered friends, to inform them about the date.

'They are going to operate,' I said, my voice shaking. 'They are going to take my foot off. I need you to come and stand by me.'

On the phone, they said supportive words, but when the time came, no one turned up. In the end, the operation was delayed by one day as the surgeons were too busy to keep the original date anyway and I communicated this to my friends and former housemates. Mr Loh visited me early in the morning on the 30th of October.

'Richard,' he said. 'We are going to do this at 11 o'clock. Is your family here?'

I shook my head.

'Friends?'

'No one has come.' The words felt sour in my mouth.

'OK,' he said. 'We're going to assign you a counsellor.'

They sent a professional from the hospital staff to comfort me, but it was not the same. Mr Loh even delayed the start of the operation by a couple of hours to see if any of my London friends or former housemates would arrive. No one did. By 1:30 p.m., the chance to wait had passed, and I was taken into the theatre completely alone.

My mind was blurry as they wheeled me in. I think I had accepted by then that I was losing the foot, but I could not imagine how my lower leg would look without my forefoot. It still somehow felt unreal.

The last thing I remember was looking up at the lights. They gave me some anaesthesia, and I fell asleep.

When I opened my eyes, the clock on the wall told me it was 4:30 p.m. The nurses came and encouraged me to drink some fluid, which at first, I refused. Eventually, I drank some water.

All the while, I had the duvet and a blanket covering me, as I was too scared to lift them and look underneath. Once I saw my new reality, there would be no escaping from it. Until I actually laid eyes on it, I could indulge in some kind of mental gymnastics and pretend it had not happened.

The lead nurse, sister Margaret, sat by the bed and tried to talk me through the situation.

'At the end of the day, Richard, you could have lost the whole leg,' she told me. 'I know it's hard, but you must try to see the positives; this is what you have, and you have to start to deal with it.'

She was extremely kind and did her best to console me, but at that time, I could not put myself into the state necessary to confront the truth. I cried intermittently and continued torturing myself, lapsing between states of anger, denial, and hopelessness. It was after 11 p.m., more than six hours after I had come out of the theatre, that I took the step I knew I must take.

Enough was enough, I decided, and in one swift movement, I threw the blankets off the bed and onto the floor. Eyes wide, I looked down at my bandaged leg, where my foot had apparently been replaced by what appeared to be a bandaged tennis ball.

I cried and cried more than I had ever cried in my life. The night doctors came in to speak to me. Much like sister Margaret, they tried to rationalise with me, and of course, what they were saying made complete sense. They explained how many people lived with these sorts of injuries and managed to have quite fulfilling lives, and the best thing to do was to accept the situation as quickly as possible and try to move on. But it was so, so hard.

The Ghanaian nurse I had met in Aspen ward came to me in the night during her break. She sat with me and encouraged me to pray. But the words felt empty. As far as I was concerned, there was no God.

That night dragged on for an eternity. I slept only fitfully. In the morning, Mr Loh returned with the doctors as they made their rounds. He was cheerful, as always.

‘Richard! How are you?’ He asked brightly. ‘Are you OK?’

‘Hello, Mr Loh.’ I did my best to smile, despite the circumstances.

‘You’ve had the operation now. Did you have a good night’s sleep?’

‘I tried,’ I told him. Mr Loh always made me want to do my best. He had such a positive aura. ‘But it was difficult.’

He asked if I had looked at the leg, so I told him everything, how hard it had been for me, how I eventually threw the blankets onto the floor. While I spoke, he nodded calmly as if everything I said was completely expected.

‘So, how do you feel now?’ He asked.

I could not help myself and began to cry, and he knelt beside the bed.

‘Don’t worry,’ he said. ‘I have always told you that we will look after you, and we will.’

He explained that the operation had been problematic and had taken three hours. They had removed my gangrenous forefoot, but they had needed to do a lot of cleaning around the wound; there was a great deal of dead tissue, even towards the rear of the foot, which they had to scoop out. Because of this, he warned me that when

I first saw my unbandaged stump, it would look very gruesome. But he assured me that there was enough live tissue there for the skin to eventually grow back. I accepted this stoically. There was nothing else I could do.

And so, the next phase of my life began. For two days, what was left of my foot remained bandaged. I was still dosed quite heavily with morphine and knew that, at some point, I would have to see the real thing.

I began eating again, mainly on Mr Loh's insistence. I used to have porridge in the mornings and force it down, even though I disliked European porridge. In Ghana, we have something similar, but it's made with millet rather than oats and tastes very different.

On the third day, Mr Loh told me they would need to change the dressing and asked if I wanted to see it. I told him I did. There was no point hiding anymore.

When the nurses came to carry out the task, I asked one of them to hold a mirror below my foot so I could see what was left. It was, of course, horrific.

There was a kind of skin flap hanging off the bottom of my leg, with a cavity behind it. At the rear of the cavity, the bone of my heel was clearly visible. Mr Loh had been right to try to prepare me. It was quite a shock. For a moment, I thought I was going to faint.

I was assured that there were procedures they could do that would encourage the live tissues and skin to regrow over the bone. Eventually, I was told, I would have a normal-looking stump.

Again, this was a point where I found myself reflecting. Back home in Ghana, the university had reopened for over a month, and my classmates were well underway in their final year. Of course, I still had much healing to do. Any thoughts of going back to join them, even just with one foot, had to be forgotten. The future I had carefully mapped out had totally disintegrated, and there was no indication of what could replace it.

Scriptures tell us that when we pray, whatever we ask for, we will receive. When we seek, we shall find.

Not for me, though. I cursed God. It is difficult to admit, but I did.

I suppose I was looking for quick answers in a situation where none were available, but I also started thinking of the person who had done this to me. Who were they? What did they think about what happened? If they could somehow appear before me and say sorry, that would mean something. That could help me to reconcile the whole episode somehow. But there was no way to make that happen.

The doctors and nurses redressed the wound and saw I was upset. I asked them to close the curtains, a request they reluctantly agreed to. After that, they left me to rest. I pulled the duvet over my head and retreated inside myself, crying long and hard. I was breaking down mentally.

Just opposite my room was another patient called Kitty. She was in the hospital to have her second leg amputated. Once I started to emerge from my internal torment, I ended up having a lovely conversation with her. She raised my spirits. I told her about my situation and everything that had happened.

Then, later in the week, I had a knock on the door and a woman walked into my room.

'Are you Richard?' She asked.

'Yes.'

'I'm Mary,' she said. 'Kitty is a very good friend of mine. Do you mind if I sit down?'

From that point on, a beautiful friendship blossomed. Mary wanted to know all about me and my family. She took such a caring interest in me and my circumstances. She gave me some money and urged me to buy a phone card to call my mother in Ghana to let her know I had had an accident and the extent of it. Up to that point, I had not spoken to my mother.

From that first visit, Mary came to see me every Tuesday. She brought me winter clothing and a cake from Harrods. Her presence lifted my spirits and helped me get through one of the worst periods imaginable. She was my only real visitor for a long time, and she has since been a significant figure in my life. She is someone I consider my mother.

Over the next few weeks, treatment on my foot continued. The doctors and nurses treated the wound using a small sponge-like material, which would be placed in the cavity and left there for a couple of days at a time. It was quite a miraculous substance, whatever it was, as every time they removed the sponge, more tissues and skin had grown. Within fourteen days, the bone was no longer visible.

This treatment continued into December when Mr Loh decided that enough skin had grown. At that point, I had to return to the operating theatre for another skin graft, using additional skin taken from my thigh.

After that, Mr Loh was happy and told me I was progressing well. This was welcome news. What he said next was not, though.

'Now you have to go home, we are going to discharge you. You are going to be an outpatient,' he told me.

CHAPTER SIX

A NEW FIGHT

My final skin graft took place in the first week of December, and my discharge was set for the week before Christmas. At first, there were some feelings of happiness. More than anything, I looked forward to eating my own food again. No more hospital shepherd's pie for me.

Practicality set in quickly, though. I needed to make arrangements. Where would I go? It would not be easy as my mobility was clearly going to be affected. The nurses had a phone on a kind of trolley, which they wheeled around for patients to use. I began making calls to anyone and everyone. No one picked up. I left messages hoping someone would call me back. No one did. At last, I got hold of Collins.

'You can't come here,' he said. He sounded shocked to hear from me. 'You can't stay with me. I don't have the time or money to look after you.'

It was painful to hear. Well, this was something else I had to reckon with besides everything I was going through. Not only had I lost my foot, but I had lost my usefulness. It seemed people now saw me as a burden. After ending the call, I cried once again.

The nurses, who were so supportive, rallied around my bed again.

'We were looking forward to you going home to your family,' they said.

'I have no family here.'

They suggested I write a letter, which was passed on to Mr Loh. As a result, social services were alerted to my situation and started coming to the hospital. They had a fixed plan in mind so that my discharge date, transport, and medication would be taken care of. They could also arrange a carer and accommodation in cases like mine. But when they looked into my circumstances, as a Ghanaian on a student visa, they said I was not entitled to support from the 'system'.

While in the hospital, I applied to extend my visa, and I also received contact from the Home Office to say my application was still being processed. That made the situation even worse. Technically, my visa had expired, meaning the authorities wanted me to return to Ghana, and the thought of this filled me with horror.

The idea of receiving support from my mother was one thing, but I also knew how terrible it would be for her. I knew that because of our family's experiences with William, the people of Nkonya Ntumda might react with superstition to my injury. There was a good chance that if I went back to Ghana, I would spend the rest of my life as an outsider.

These complications meant my discharge was delayed, and I found myself still in the hospital over Christmas. My guardian angel, Mary, came to my aid again and arranged for me to spend Christmas Day with her at her house. The hospital provided a wheelchair with which she and her sister Margaret took me home in Mary's car. Margaret lived nearby.

I really enjoyed that! Even though English food had been a problem for me, the turkey was delicious. Mary insisted I try broccoli, but I had no idea how to eat this weird, bushy, green vegetable. I had to make the effort.

After the meal, Mary wheeled me aside and gave me a talking to.

'Try not to cry about this thing,' she said. 'We have all had problems, but you can fight this. We will support you.' She told me a personal and painful story about herself, which made me realise that what she said was true. There was more to me than two feet. I still had my brain, and I still had my spirit.

Mary and her sister, Margaret, showed me such incredible love, and despite everything I was going through, they made the Christmas of 1998 a little bit special. How inspiring it was to be the recipient of such kindness!

Just after 6 p.m., they drove me back to the hospital, and immediately, it seemed, all my problems crowded back in. It felt like I had reached the end of my welcome there, not from the staff who had always been wonderful and remained so, but from the system. The system had a problem with me because I did not fit neatly into its channels.

They were trying to house me, but there were problems at every turn. The Home Office refused my application for a visa extension. Nobody knew how this thing would end.

New Year came, which I spent at the hospital. Mary came again to visit me. Once more, I appreciated her time, and her presence truly lifted my spirits, but the situation regarding my future was becoming tense. The discussion had now moved toward deporting me against my wishes, something I intended to resist with all my might. Mr Loh and his team wrote to support my application to stay in the country. Inside me, I was still determined to lift my family up. I knew that if I returned to Ghana as a disabled person, that would never happen. Somehow, I had to stay in the UK. It was my only chance.

In the meantime, I practised walking, at first with a frame. The wound was still extremely sore, so it was challenging, but I knew I had to try. The skin was not fully attached, meaning it was painful when I put my weight on it, but there was no way I wanted to be dependent on a wheelchair to get around.

I appealed the Home Office decision, and they extended my visa to the end of February while my case was under review. Early in February, I was told accommodation had been found for me in a village in Kent. I had never heard of the place, so I phoned Mary for advice.

'There is no way you are going there,' she said firmly.

'Why?'

'The Medway area is the heart of British National Party territory. You will have a hard enough time with your physical problems. The last thing you need is to confront rampant racism too.'

'OK,' I replied. That was reason enough for me. But Mary had not finished.

'It's also too far for me to drive on a regular basis,' she said. 'I want to see you often and make sure you are OK.'

Following Mary's advice, I wrote a letter explaining that I did not want to be housed in Kent. Mr Loh read it and offered his support. Early in March, seven months after my accident, I was told they had found me alternative housing in Wood Green, in the borough of Haringey in North London. Again, I phoned Mary, and this time, she gave me the thumbs up.

Once the date for my departure was set, I became nervous. I had lived in the hospital for such a long time. Ever since the moment my life changed, all I had known was my room there and the friendly faces of the staff. This would be a new challenge altogether; the real world, where people were not paid to be nice to me. How would society cope with my presence?

The staff were incredible, as they had been all the way through. They bought gifts and items to help with my transition to living alone, practical things like bedsheets, pressing iron, and cooking utensils, which I would need.

The hospital administration, however, was not so helpful. It emerged that their records stated that I was a private patient. As a result, the administrator, a blonde lady in a business suit, came to see me in my room. She listed all the procedures I had been through, including the many hours I had spent in the operating theatre, and rent for my room with a fixed smile on her face.

'As you are aware,' she said, 'You are not entitled to free treatment.' With that, she handed me an itemised bill. It totalled more than one hundred thousand Pounds (£100,000)

I immediately handed it back to her. 'Have you finished?' I asked. 'I have got a few things to say.'

She nodded.

'Firstly, you say I'm not entitled, but I am, and I will tell you why. I am a citizen of the Commonwealth, and the UK is part of the Commonwealth. Secondly, I have been working in this country and had contributed to or paid

National Insurance. I did not come to this country as an illegal immigrant. I came on a working visa, worked, and paid into the system. Thirdly, any person involved in an accident, regardless of his national status, must be looked after. I was involved in an accident and was rushed to this hospital. I did not walk in as a private patient. For these reasons, I do not think it is right, in any circumstance, to chase me around with this bill. Your news is a source of great stress to me, and for that, I'll have to seek the services of a solicitor to write to the hospital.'

I do not know where I found those words then, but that is what I said. The administrator turned red in the face. She did not know what to say but managed an apology and walked out. On the way out, she stopped at the nurse's station and must have told the nurses what I had said.

As soon as the administrator left the ward, the nurses crowded into my room, clapping and cheering.

'Richard,' one of them asked, 'How did you have all this knowledge?'

I smiled and shrugged. They kissed me and told me how happy they were. None of them thought it was fair that I had been billed.

By 1:30 p.m., a hospital director had come to my room to apologise, which felt like a real victory. It gave me a sense of belief in the future. As Mary had said, I may only have had one foot, but that did not mean I was incapable.

The day I checked out of Barnet Hospital, Mary, Margaret, and Margaret's husband, Frank, insisted on taking me to my new place, so an ambulance was not needed. They came with two cars and loaded everything. My private room at the hospital had become my home and so I had all my belongings there.

I had been allocated a small studio flat, and everybody was generous with their time in helping me set it up. Mary stayed until around 8 p.m. that day, but when it got late, she had to bid me goodnight. She wished me well and left.

'This is it now,' I thought. 'This is when everything begins.'

CHAPTER SEVEN

MAKING IT WORK

When I awoke the following morning, I looked out of my window into the garden. It was a bright, clear day. Then I made my way to the front door and opened it. I could see people out on the street, moving around, going about their business. Loneliness gnawed at me. I suddenly felt very weak.

I had no phone, so I was unable to call anyone. I went back in and closed the curtains, thinking it would be better to shut the world out for a while. I ate some cereal. Then at some point during the day, I realised a note had been pushed under my door.

The note was handwritten and said that someone called Ade (pseudonym) had been to see me with his manager. Apparently, they would come back soon.

Ade, it turned out, was my appointed carer from a local nursing agency. When we met, I was happy to see that he was black, like me, which made me feel comfortable. I was allotted four hours a week of Ade's time, during which he would clean the flat and do my shopping.

I was provided with vouchers, with which I could buy groceries for my first week, and told that when they ran out, I needed to collect the next batch myself from Barnet council. That would then become a fortnightly ritual.

Things began well with Ade. He went into Wood Green with my vouchers and bought me some food. He was confident and easy to get on with. It did strike me, however, that he seemed an unusual type to be working as a carer. He was young, tall, and handsome. He had a bit of charisma about him and clearly liked designer clothes. After the first few visits, he took me shopping with him, so I could have more input into how my vouchers were spent. I discovered then that he drove a Mercedes with a pumping stereo system. This did not seem like a car that someone on a carer's salary would drive. Something seemed a little off about all this, but I did not dwell on it because, at first, I liked him.

Toward the end of the first week, the District Nurse came to complete an assessment. She was very kind and told me she would get me a 'Freedom Pass,' which allowed me free travel on public transport.

That was crucial, as without that, I had no way to make the six-mile journey to Barnet to collect my vouchers.

So, the first weeks passed, and I managed by cocooning myself in my little studio apartment. Apart from Ade, the District Nurse and Mary, who came to visit, I did not see anyone else. Eventually, with my brand-new travel card, I had to venture out. I used a walking stick and took the bus to Barnet to collect my allocation of vouchers.

As I prepared to go to Barnet Council, I realised, with horror, that I had nothing to wear over my stump. I ended up putting wool socks over the dressing and hopped along on my crutches. I noticed people on and off the bus were staring at me which made me feel a bit uncomfortable.

My first few months continued in this way. Mary visited me regularly, but in general, I was something of a hermit, living in my own little world. A woman called Sandra lived upstairs, she was a heavy smoker and often had drug users visiting. One time, when I made my fortnightly pilgrimage to Barnet, my flat was broken into and some of my things stolen. I suspected one of Sandra's friends was responsible, but had no evidence. That shook me up. But other than that, it was a quiet and fairly isolated existence.

During this period, I was also scheduled to go for my first appointment to have a prosthetic foot fitted. Coincidentally, it was the Royal National Orthopaedic Hospital, where I used to work as a cleaner. My first journey there in a taxi was strange. It arrived on Brockley Hill, where the speeding car which hit me had come from, and dropped me at the very doors I had walked out of before my accident. It was the first time I was there after the accident. I felt strangely numb.

My sense of deja vu amplified when I went to meet Dr Marks, the prosthetics expert, who worked in the exact room I remembered so well. These appointments became a regular thing for me, as my travails with prosthetics would go on for years. I developed a technique of turning my head as I arrived, meaning I never looked at the spot where I was run over, because it brought back memories of the ill-fated day. I guess, in a way, I was avoiding a replay of my trauma.

Meanwhile, I began to develop reservations about Ade. Packages began arriving at the flat, addressed to fictitious names. Every time a package arrived, within a few minutes, Ade, or sometimes one of his associates, would turn up.

'Oh, that's for me,' they would say. 'I had this thing sent here.'

This began to happen frequently and made me uneasy. What was Ade doing having packages sent to my address using fake names? I knew it had to be something questionable.

While all this was happening, Mary and I frequently discussed my future, particularly my education. We had talked about this a great deal in the hospital, and she knew it was important to me to obtain my degree, and then pursue a career. She also knew that my dream was to go to LSE.

'You have to go back to school,' she would say. 'I don't know how we will manage it, but we will find a way.'

We obtained the transcript of my results from the University of Ghana and made tentative contact with LSE. They were impressed enough with my academic record to offer me a place, which was very encouraging, but they stipulated that if I joined them, I would have to repeat the second year. The other glaring issue was that, as an overseas student, I would have to pay. The fees, of course, were completely unaffordable.

Mary and I discussed it and decided to look for another institution, hoping conditions might be more favourable elsewhere. We tried Middlesex—a university with various sites around North London, which would be easier for me to get to—where I looked forward to reading Politics and International Studies at their campus in Tottenham. This was just down the road from my flat in Wood Green, so appeared a decent option.

I attended an interview and completed an assessment test, after which I was offered a place, into the third and final year, as I wanted. This was such a happy day, but there remained the ever-present issue of money. Middlesex was not as expensive as LSE, but I would still somehow need to find four thousand Pounds (£4,000) a year to finish my degree.

I was able to start the course in lieu of payment, and things began well. I quickly made some great friends, but about six weeks in, I received my first bill, which I obviously could not pay. Luckily, by this time, the course tutors had become quite attached to me, as I was passionate and knowledgeable about the subjects being covered. As a result, a strange compromise was made. Until the bill was settled, I was not prevented from attending lectures or seminars but simply disallowed from accessing university resources, particularly the library. I circumvented this by getting friends to borrow books for me.

It was another difficult period, but, as always, I managed to survive.

One day, at home, leafing through my personal documents, I found a policy for travel insurance. I had completely forgotten that I had taken this out before flying to the UK and immediately spoke to Mary. Mary put me in touch with a solicitor, who discovered I was just within the deadline to make a claim. Miraculously, I was entitled to a pay out of five and a half thousand Pounds (£5,500), which covered my university fees for the year, with a little bit to spare.

With that, the situation stabilised, but I continued to be troubled by Ade and his mysterious packages. Ade never spoke to me about it directly but did offer hints. On one occasion, he asked if I wanted to make a little money by storing parcels for him and passing them on.

'Look, if you want to make money in this country, this is how,' he said. Although my financial situation was quite desperate, I did not consider it for a second. By then, I suspected Ade was moving drugs, so I thanked him but declined politely. Involvement in anything like that went completely against the moral code I held all my life.

Then one day, a package arrived which was extremely large and heavy. It was also different because, unlike the others, it had my name on it. As it was addressed to me, I took a knife and carved it open. To my surprise, the box was full of expensive-looking Canon cameras.

As usual, within a few minutes, there was a knock at my door. I opened it to be confronted with a guy I had not seen before. He introduced himself as a friend of Ade and told me the package was for him.

'But I don't know you,' I said. 'And the package was addressed to me in any event'.

Immediately the guy pulled a gun from inside his jacket. 'Don't mess me around,' he said, scowling. 'I'll blow your head off.' My legs became like jelly. I started shaking and sweating and could not utter a word.

I hurriedly passed over the box, but that was the last straw. In truth, Ade had not been a particularly good carer anyway. He often neglected his basic duties, and my flat was not even clean half the time. As the situation had become so uncomfortable, I decided to make a change.

I wrote a letter to the agency requesting a change of carer and did not go into detail, but I made it very clear that I did not want Ade to come again. This proved to be one of the best decisions I ever made.

It was a relief not to see Ade or any of the hangers-on who came with him anymore, and after about a week, my new carer arrived. I opened the door to find a lovely smile waiting for me.

'Are you Richard?' My new female carer asked.

'I am,' I said. Immediately, I was so pleased to see her.

'I'm Diane.'

She was dressed casually, in jeans and a leather jacket, but I could tell she had a lovely figure. There was something so warm and soothing about her face, and from the moment Diane first set foot in my flat, I felt so at home with her. Up to this point, my life outside of the hospital had felt very challenging, and although I retained my sense of determination, I was beset with doubt. Could I really make this work? Could I function in the world after the accident? Perhaps, most importantly, could I truly be happy like this?

After Diane came into my life, those doubts began to subside. I came to think of her as the third of my guardian angels, after Mary and Mfon. She was of Guyanese heritage and had such an easy-going manner.

She looked around and was shocked by the state of my flat. The bathroom horrified her, and she spent over four hours cleaning the place, far longer than she was supposed to stay for the day. She also noted that my clothes and bedsheets did not seem to have been washed for a very long time. When she finished her work in the flat, she took everything to the laundry for me. Suddenly, it was as if someone was really taking care of me.

On one of her earliest visits, Mary had just left, having brought me some food and drinks from McDonald's, I shared the food with Diane, who gave me a cheeky smile. By this time, I had a landline telephone installed in the flat. That evening, in her own time, Diane called me to see if I was OK.

The next time she came, she brought some Dettol and lemon.

'I'm not happy with how they have been cleaning your wound,' she said. 'I'm going to make sure it is done properly.'

This was outside of her remit as a carer. Certainly, Ade had never taken any interest in how my foot was healing. It was only the district nurses who did anything like that. Soon, the wound began to feel much better. Diane also started bringing me home-cooked Caribbean food that she had made herself. It felt to me that something special was developing between us.

Diane had been looking after me for a couple of months when she brought her sister Marva to visit. Marva was as lovely as her sister, and it was evident, by this point, that things had progressed beyond a typical professional relationship.

'Me and Marva had an idea,' Diane said, with that mischievous twinkle in her eye.

'Go on,' I replied suspiciously.

'We thought it would be nice if we all went out.'

They invited me to come with them to a pub in Soho, where bands and DJs were playing. It felt so wonderful for them to include me in something like that. By this time, I had not had a social life for around a year. I had a wonderful time, although there was some sadness too. My leg hurt throughout the evening, and while Diane, Marva, and their friends often got up from the table to dance, I could not join them.

From there, things continued to develop between us. It seemed it was personally important to Diane to help to rehabilitate me back into society as fully as possible. She started bringing me new clothes, even a suit and by now, our connection had evolved into a proper, romantic relationship. Slowly but surely, I was becoming more myself again.

CHAPTER EIGHT

THE BALL STARTS ROLLING

Through a combination of luck and the help of others, I managed to finish university. Through one of my acquaintances, I managed to get a job in a warehouse in Wood Green for a while to earn extra money. It was supposed to be a data entry job, but it involved a lot of walking, so it did not last long. Nonetheless, I managed to save enough to buy myself a computer.

I was awarded a good 2.1 (upper second-class honours) degree in 2000 from Middlesex University. It was a happy time, and I began to receive visits from Ghanaian friends who had come on holidays, even having some staying with me.

My dark days of fear and isolation seemed to be well and truly over.

I applied to study for a Masters degree at Westminster University, but once again, money was a barrier. I needed to find the course fees, having exhausted all my previous funds when completing my previous course. Again, one of my guardian angels came to my rescue. A few days before the course was due to start, Mfon phoned me. She wanted to know if I had enrolled for the course.

‘I don’t have the deposit,’ I told her. ‘I applied for multiple scholarships and help from charities, but all of them had turned me down.’

‘Come and see me,’ Mfon said. ‘Let’s talk about it.’

By this time, Mfon was working at Queen Mary’s Hospital in Paddington. I went to meet her and stayed overnight at her place. In the morning, by the time I got out of bed, she had left for the bank and came back with two thousand, six hundred and fifty Pounds (£2,650), the amount I needed for my deposit to start the course.

‘I want you to take this money, my brother’ she said. ‘Take a cab, go down there now, and register for the course this morning.’

And so, I started to study for my Master’s. The travelling to and from Westminster, then around the campus, was problematic and caused much discomfort to my leg. Diane would help whenever she could, sometimes going with me to the university, then waiting and helping me home if it did not interfere with her own work.

By the time my first semester results came, my second instalment was due. Again, I could not afford the two thousand Pounds (£2,000). This time, and for my subsequent instalments, Diane paid my tuition fees, meaning my degree had been entirely funded by friends.

All the help that I received from people truly made me reflect. Although the accident and its aftermath had been terrible, I was fortunate that people had been so kind. The fact that others were prepared to do these things for me helped to restore some of my faith in God. I was becoming a believer again and thought I could recognise God's hand in what was happening.

Thoughts soon turned to my post-university life, which intensified when NTL (later to become Virgin) came to the University for a recruitment drive. This excited me. The opportunity to work for a large, international company could be the key to achieving my ambitions.

I entered their process as one of the hundreds of student applicants all over the country, passed the different stages of the recruitment process, and was invited to the final step at Warwick University, near Coventry. After passing that stage, I was provisionally offered a position, on the proviso that my right to live and work in the UK was verified. Sadly, from there, things once again got very complicated.

I completed the necessary forms but could not provide my right to live and work in the UK, and then eagerly awaited the outcome. I could not wait to start work. I got home one day after a trip to the shops and, a message was waiting for me on my answerphone. NTL said that after reviewing my application carefully, they could not obtain a work permit for me and for that reason, they could not offer me a position.

I was distraught and even shed a few tears. I wanted to earn some good money and repay the people who had helped me. I wanted to begin to make my way in the world, to fulfil my destiny and leave the horrors of the past behind.

Diane came to see me. I could not stand to see her upset.

'I refuse to give up,' I told her. 'If they won't employ me, I will establish my own company.'

'But you don't have any papers. How can you?',
Diane asked me.

Before graduation, I met a recruitment consultant with an office in Tottenham. I spoke to her about her business. She recruited nurses and supplied them to hospitals and care homes that needed them, which planted a seed in my mind. 'I could do this better than her,' I thought. A recruitment company would need minimal start-up costs – just an office and telephone. From there, it had almost limitless potential.

I phoned a business advisory centre in Tottenham and found they had an extremely go-ahead attitude. After talking to a gentleman called Shiraz Kiyani, he asked if I wanted to register a company. Adrenaline surged through my system.

'Yes!' I answered.

'OK, great. What is it?'

'What is what?

‘The company name you want to register. What is it?’

I paused for a moment. ‘Hold on,’ I said. ‘I’ll call you back.’

I phoned a cousin of mine, Prosper, who had also come to London by this time. I told him my idea that I wanted to recruit nurses and teachers and that I had just spoken to someone at the business advisory centre in Tottenham who was ready to help. I also contacted my nephew, Albert who was in London too by then.

‘But you don’t have any papers,’ Prosper said.

‘I don’t think I need them!’ I replied. By this point, a kind of youthful spirit had come over me, and I was too wrapped up in my excitement to see sense. ‘But I need a name.’

Prosper and Albert came to my flat to discuss things, and I used the intervening time to jot down ideas. By the time they arrived, I had a piece of paper covered in scribblings. After much frantic debate, we decided to focus on the education sector and settled on the name Winstons Teaching Services, which we liked because we thought it sounded very English.

Once that was decided, I phoned the advisory centre and gave them the name. They told us to come in for a meeting, so we went down there on a few occasions for business advice and to seek help to register the company. We were warned that we would need to be patient. Mr Kiyani said, ‘I can see the desire and enthusiasm burning in your stomach. That will take you very far, but you must be patient.

Things will not happen overnight'. Our advisor reckoned it would take three-to-six months to get our first client.

We made some flyers and installed a phone line in my studio flat at Lordship Lane in Wood Green. And then within a few days, something magical happened.

Prosper, Albert, and I were just young, silly boys with no business acumen, yet a few days after we had delivered our flyers, the phone started ringing nonstop. What no one had accounted for was that, at the time, there was a serious shortage of teachers in London, and schools were crying out for extra staff. Of course, we had no teachers on our books, as we had just established ourselves, but Prosper had trained as a teacher back in Ghana.

'Don't worry!' He shouted. 'Don't worry, we can do this!'

Prosper also knew some other Ghanaian teachers living in the UK, so he started calling all of them. By our second proper week of business, we already had several teachers out on the job. When we reported back to the advisory centre about what was happening, Mr Kiyani advised that we needed an office because with so much work coming in, he did not think it was appropriate to be trading out of my flat. We were connected to the Prince's Trust, who gave us a grant and a loan, with which we rented an office in Tottenham Green Enterprise Centre. Although it felt that we had hit the ground running and were three young executives about to make their mark in the world, we soon realised that the high demand for our services brought its own problems.

Very quickly, we began receiving negative reports from schools about our teachers. They were poorly prepared, they could not manage the classes, and so on. Our frantic rush to put people in place had meant our quality control was lacking, and we had literally just sent out anyone we could find. As quickly as we had picked it up, we soon began losing business.

After a few months, Prosper, Albert, and I discussed things again. The teaching world was clearly a minefield. We decided we needed to change tack, and after a quick brainstorm, settled on supplying nurses instead. We changed the company name to Winstons Human Resources Ltd. and started over again.

This time, however, the original advice we received held true. Nothing happened for months, literally nothing. We tried everything we could, working the phones like mad and sending out flyers again, but we could not get a single client. It reached the point that the money we received from the Prince's Trust was nearly exhausted. Diane supported me almost entirely, providing my meals and buying me clothes. Without her, I would have been in big trouble.

We learned of a man who ran a successful agency in a similar field in North London. He was a pastor too called Godson Lawal, and we were advised it would be good to approach him for advice. Prosper and I were nearly broke by this point, so it seemed necessary to roll the dice.

We went to his office, which was in Edmonton, near Tottenham. He was not there the first time we visited, but a colleague kindly gave us his phone number. We called him, and he seemed very happy to hear from two enthusiastic Ghanaian boys. We saw him the following day, and after a good chat, he offered us his help. He said he would subcontract some work to us through his business.

Before long, he invited us to join his company to bid for a place on a National Health Service Framework agreement for the Southeast of England. This was a particularly large framework involving all the NHS Trusts in the Southeast. We were absolutely thrilled when we got a place on the framework. Now it was time to approach the individual Trusts to do a presentation for an award of contract. Our first port of call was Kingston Hospital NHS Trust in South London.

Pastor Lawal taught us the rudiments of business, especially customer relations, and that knowledge has remained with me all these years, thanks to his many years of experience in the business.

Our previous encounter with the Prince's Trust also taught me a great business lesson too: we were asked to put a business plan together with the cash flow forecast and then grilled to justify our figures, which we did with some difficulty. This meant I knew what to expect in Kingston. It went well, and as soon as we left, they called us in the car to say we had won the contract.

When the contract finally arrived at our office, with our company name on it, it was a wonderful moment. We were up and running.

We went through the same process at Ashford and St Peter's NHS Trust and Royal Surrey County Hospital NHS Trust. Pastor Lawal showed us the ropes in terms of recruiting and vetting nurses, and suddenly, we were turning over a decent amount of money a month.

There was one problem, though – all the while, our new mentor kept control of the invoicing as we had bid for the contract together, which meant that after about three months of solid, productive activity, we had still not seen any money. Pastor Lawal was in the meantime paying all the staff we supplied to the hospitals.

Prosper and I could not afford to continue like that, so we went to his office to discuss the issue. We tried not to offend him, but when we explained how we felt, he was not impressed. Later, I realised that it takes the NHS time to set up contractors before any payment starts coming to the supplier. In hindsight, we probably did not approach the matter correctly. It was the case that the client had not started making payments.

'You know what, boys? he said dismissively, in a very calm voice. 'I've made my money already. Take everything and hopefully, you can make a success out of this.'

He decided he did not want to be involved anymore and that we could take over all aspects of the business. Despite this, Pastor Lawal continued to mentor me and twenty-two years on he remains in my life.

While that felt like a big win in some ways, we now had to come up with a way to raise invoices. We had no system for this, no software of any kind. Again, we asked the business advisory service for advice, who suggested we get 'QuickBooks,' an accounting software package available from various retailers.

Again, I borrowed the money from Diane for QuickBooks and installed it immediately. It took us a few hours to get used to it, but it meant we could start invoicing straight away. Nonetheless, it took nearly four weeks for us to receive our first cheque for twelve thousand Pounds (£12,000). In the meantime, we had agreed to pay our nurses fortnightly, so we had to find the money to fulfil this promise. It was a challenge, but at least things were up and running.

From that point, things just seemed to expand over the next few months. But as they did, our costs rose exponentially too. It was clear there was huge potential in the business, but it was also true that to realise that potential, investment was needed. I racked my brains. The level of finance required was too much to ask of Diane. Besides, by this point, a little distance had grown between us. Diane was ten years older than me and unable to have any more children.

For me, this was a major issue. I loved Diane very much, and her intervention in my life was crucial in many ways. Yet fatherhood is a hugely important element of Ghanaian culture and something I could not miss out on; for my family, especially my parents, I needed to continue the family line. This caused me a lot of inner conflicts, but as a result, Diane and I eventually split, which caused her considerable distress and sent her into a depression, for which I felt so guilty.

However, through mutual friends, I met and then married another woman called Lena. Like me, Lena was very ambitious and had worked as a banker in Ghana before coming to England to pursue a Master's degree. We had a great deal in common, and everything went from there.

Shortly after the wedding, which was a small affair, as I grappled with the pressure of securing financing for my company, and being able to pay the nurses, I found myself on a bus in the Bruce Grove area in Tottenham in North London. Suddenly, a voice spoke to me. 'Go to Barclays and get a loan,' it said. I did not know where the voice had come from, but something about it was deeply compelling.

So, I got off the bus and went to the bank. They were preparing to close for the day, and I was the last customer to enter.

'How can I help you, sir?' The female staff asked.

'I need a loan.'

'For what?'

'I've just got married, and I cannot afford to take my wife on honeymoon.'

The clerk's face opened in joy. 'What a romantic thing!' She exclaimed.

She said I needed to wait while other customers were dealt with first. Then, when my time came, she entered my details into the computer system to see if my request for fifteen thousand Pounds (£15,000) could be met.

'You don't really qualify, you know,' she said. 'But I will do everything I personally can to ensure you get this loan.' She made a couple of phone calls and asked me to wait.

Less than ten minutes later, I had fifteen thousand Pounds (£15,000) in my account, which made me think again about my faith in God. Whose voice had I heard on the bus? Who was creating all of these fortunate coincidences?

Maybe He was guiding me, after all.

CHAPTER NINE

THE HOSTILE ENVIRONMENT

While my business ventures were gathering early momentum, I faced a very frustrating fight over my status as a UK resident. For a long time, there was a great deal of uncertainty.

I had applied for leave to remain on compassionate grounds, as I was still rehabilitating and receiving medical care. However, the case had not moved forward on that basis at all.

While I was still with Diane, I met with a lawyer called Stephen Cockings. He thought that as I was Diane's 'common law husband' there could be some leeway in terms of my residency status. Again, this did not really work out, but Cockings was able to secure me a two-year extension, which gave me some breathing space. Around this time, I moved to Finchley, as there was too much crime in the Wood Green area and shortly after the move, I received my temporary residency visa, which needed to be renewed in 2006.

I also learned to drive, despite the impediment caused by my disability, which was significant progress. However, this caused unexpected consequences in other parts of my life. By this time, I had been visiting the Royal National Orthopaedic Hospital regularly for years and felt that I was coping with returning there. For some unexplained reason though, when I started to drive there, I found myself in a very heightened state of emotions and apprehension. The first time I drove past where I had been knocked over, I looked at the exact spot where I lay gasping for water and I dissolved in tears. Something within compelled me to look at the spot where the car had hit me. Maybe it was because I had just driven past it myself, but it had a huge emotional impact on me. I knew then that I still needed to process my trauma. There was so much about what had happened to me that I had buried.

To advance my residency case, I had been visiting the office of Barbara Roche, the Labour MP for Wood Green. In fact, she got so fed up with my constant presence that, after a while, she stopped offering me a seat in the hope that she could get rid of me quickly. I wrote to the Home Secretary John Reid and Tony Blair, the Prime Minister at the time.

At one point in 2006, the darkest moment of the whole saga, I received a letter saying my application had been denied, and I had just 14 days to leave the country. Cockings then referred me to an immigration judge with his own law firm, David Webb. Mr Webb's office was down in the City of London, and I made several trips to discuss my case with him. This period was very unsettling.

It was expensive, and even just one consultation with Mr Webb would cost me a couple of hundred pounds. At the time, it felt like there was little choice. I knew if I was deported, all my hard work would be in vain.

By December 2004, Lena and I were able to buy a house in Harlow. Our first child, Jason, was born in 2005, but when the renewal of my temporary visa was again rejected in 2006, Lena lost faith. She had become frustrated with the uncertainty over my future, had finished her Master's, and had a job offer in Ghana. After long and thoughtful discussions, we agreed that Lena would go back to Ghana to take the job. This was not an attempt to abandon me, but that was a fallback plan so that in case everything else failed, I would at least have a wife who would be the breadwinner of the family. I knew, because of my status, there was a chance I would end up in Ghana soon too, and this was an emotional blow to me. The day I drove my wife and son to the airport and returned home alone, I cried.

I stayed to fight the case and saw Bill Rammell, the Conservative MP for Harlow. He looked down his nose at me 'I'm not here to help illegal immigrants stay in the country,' he said. 'I am not illegal but under immigration control', I replied. I debated the difference between the two statements until he backed down. What have I got to lose? Nothing. Richard, make your point, it is your only chance, I thought. The worse he could have done was to walk me out of his surgery. I was down anyway and could not have fallen any further. I was not prepared to be easily dismissed.

I explained my situation and made it clear that I was in business and not claiming benefits and that I was somebody trapped in the system. Making progress under such a condition was near impossible. At least we both knew where we stood after the little debate.

It took a lot of talking, but eventually, he agreed to write a letter to the Home Office on my behalf. It did not seem to do any good, but at least I got a reply from the Home Office.

At this point, I changed my solicitor to another specialist immigration firm called Del & Co. Solicitors, run by Dele Olawanle. He read all the details of my case and was incensed.

'We will fight this all the way!' he declared. 'Even if we have to go to the European Court of Human Rights.'

Del & Co's representation to the Home Office and 10 Downing Street was a game changer. Mr Olawanle told me that his first port of call would be to contact Prime Minister Tony Blair. I told him I had already tried that route, but he thought it was worth another go. Letters and replies came and went for a while, and although it felt good to have a passionate advocate like Dele Olawanle on my side, I still could not see any clear signs of progress coming anytime soon.

But shortly after, Tony Blair's office contacted me for further details, and there was continued contact with the Home Office after Dele & Co. had contacted Downing

Street. Tellingly, the final correspondence from the Home Office was apologetic. It seemed they recognised they had not treated my case with the sympathy it deserved, particularly in light of my accident and continued treatment. They admitted my application should have been reviewed properly back in 2002 and that this had not happened because of an oversight on their part. That, finally, felt like progress.

They were suddenly talking to me like a human being.

At last, late in July of 2007, I received a phone call from Mr Olawanle out of the blue while picking up Diane's sister from the airport.

'Richard!' he said, in his friendly Nigerian tone. 'Are you sitting down?'

'Yes. I'm at the airport waiting for someone.'

'There is some good news.'

I thought he would tell me they had extended my visa for another year or two.

'Richard,' he said. 'They have asked if you can send your passport to them. You have been given permanent residence.'

I could not believe what I was hearing, and the drive back from the airport was one of the happiest of my life. This was nine years after I arrived in the country, and I had been fighting the system all this time to have my immigration status regularised. Diane's sister must have thought I was on drugs because I was so happy.

Soon afterwards, I went down to Del & Co's office in Haringey. We filled in the necessary forms together and sent my passport off.

A couple of weeks later, they returned my passport with all the necessary stamps and accreditations.

It felt as if the weight of the world had just been lifted from my shoulders. Finally, I could travel to Ghana to see my wife and son, without fear of being disallowed re-entry to the UK. It was such a relief. I had missed them so much and I could not wait. Lena was very happy when I phoned her with the good news. She sang songs of praise as I have never heard sung. I told Mary, Diane, and Mfon, and then flew to Ghana in October 2007. I spent three weeks there, with my family and it was so wonderful to see Jason running around the house.

My mother was ecstatic to see me. But because I did not allow her to see my leg or tell her the full extent of the injuries, she said, 'I thought your situation was worse than this'. I thank God you are here.

Just after I received my residency, a clampdown started on security companies. The Home Office had set up the Security Industry Authority (SIA) task force to weed out illegal immigrants from the security industry. By this time, we had incorporated a company called Winstons Security Ltd, which provided manned guarding services to companies in London and the Southeast. Soon another company called WinClaims Ltd was also established, to provide claims management services. The SIA had written to Winstons Security Ltd to confirm whether the directors have the right to live and work in the UK within fourteen days. I produced the necessary documents which saved the business. If I had not received my right to live and work in the UK, the company could have been closed down by the SIA.

CHAPTER TEN

THE THIRD BATTLE

In 2006, I received a boost in my finances when the Motor Insurance Bureau paid me one hundred and nineteen thousand Pounds (£119,000) after legal expenses.

That money was an enormous help and went a long way to stabilise my businesses. I was finally able to pay back Diane and Mfon and built a house for my mother back in Nkonya Ntumda. That was a huge moment and the realisation of a long held goal.

After that, I focused again on the future. Lena and I ended up separating a couple of years after the birth of our second child, Anne-Lois, and subsequently divorced. On the business side, we had run into some trouble with supplying nurses due to new regulatory issues which had been introduced. So, we decided to move into security. We would recruit and supply security guards to anyone who needed them.

We moved offices from Tottenham to Enfield and reincorporated ourselves as Winstons Security Services Ltd. We employed an American associate, an ex-Marine, and decided to Americanise our company image. The uniforms were imported from the United States, which we thought would help to differentiate us in the market. However, the shift in direction prompted a period of stasis. Nine long months passed a single client, and although I could sustain things with the insurance money, I knew this could not last forever.

By 2008, the money had basically run out, and it was time to face the future without Prosper. The year before we had gone to HSBC bank and taken out a sixty thousand Pounds (£60,000) loan which we spent on Winstons Security. The money was spent on branding and 'Americanising' the service we provided. Little did we know that the market was not ready for that.

Prosper for personal reasons decided to relocate to Ghana where we had established an office for WinClaims. This meant I would be running Winstons Security and he would be managing the business in Ghana. The business was doing well in Ghana but, our relationship became strained and eventually completely broke down. I decided that I could not stay in a relationship that had become so acerbic and toxic. The relationship was not good for my health, I told Pastor Lawal, in one of my meetings with him. I, therefore, decided I would have to move on and chart a new path for myself.

When Prosper left and Winstons was wound down in 2010, I established a new company, Guarding Professionals Ltd, and took on the debt of Winstons Security. The reason was that I had provided a personal guarantee for the liabilities of Winstons Security. This meant I took on the HSBC liability with me and my insurance money which I had risked on the business.

Despite that, I used the experience I had accrued to establish my new business and drove it forward successfully. I travelled all over the country, Birmingham, Bristol, Manchester, and Liverpool trying to build the business.

It took a while but one way or the other I was determined to win. Before long, I began picking up clients, and the business grew. As with any venture, there were threats along the way. In 2012, a client breached its contract with my company. I decided to take the client on. I won the legal argument, and I received a payment in the region of ten thousand Pounds (£10,000).

This victory was one of my motivations for starting law school in the same year. It was something I had thought about for a long time and the thought crystalised during my dealings with lawyers throughout my immigration case. The legal profession is not only lucrative but also a worthy one if practised properly.

During this same period, I met a lady called Joan Asare. We had known each other for many years, and our friendship gradually blossomed into a romance. Her presence in my life was invaluable, as, once again, I found myself in a transitional phase; having built the first business and then letting it go, establishing the second took much energy and support and so the relationship was timely.

Joan really understood my situation from day one. She is always patient with me and allowed me space if I needed it. Sometimes, at the end of a long day and with my leg causing me pain, I became irritable. The pain was not localised in what remained of my foot but spread up my shin and even into my back. Because the injury affected my movements and gait, it had knock-on effects all around my body. Joan got this and could cope with it very well. She knew when to give me space and allow me time to rest. That was very important and meant our relationship had a much more secure foundation.

Joan always had a way of knowing what was best for me. She insisted I buy an exercise bike to use in the house. My limited mobility had the potential to create other health problems in time, so she encouraged me to be physically active. This proved to be a great move for me, and soon I bought a road bike too, which I could use around the streets of my local area.

With Joan's continued encouragement, I completed my law qualification in 2016, which proved a well-timed move, as by then, I was about to embark on what I think of as my third great battle. Up to this point in my life, I had endured two noteworthy fights to be where I wanted to be. The first resulted from my injury and what it did to my body and mind. In fact, these two battles raged on concurrently. Whilst fighting my health problems, I found myself fighting the system to remain in the UK.

Now, with my second business growing and my qualification to practice law confirmed, I faced a fight that threatened to ruin me. I had no choice but to engage in it, or face the loss of my livelihood, my house, and everything.

My problems began from within, as an employee of mine began sabotaging the business; we lost contract after contract. Everything was a mess; there were payments uncollected and invoices not filed.

One client, I discovered, owed us fifty seven thousand Pounds (£57,000) because of this employee's negligence. It was disappointing as he was a Ghanaian that I had helped with work when he needed it and he had managed things for me while I was busy with my law qualification, but I suspect he had become jealous of my success. A fact that you have to come to terms with in business is that sometimes other people let you down. The truth is that I was tired at this time and started losing my sense of direction and focus. I was burnt out and I needed a boost.

This point was made to me very clearly, as soon as I began to run into trouble with my biggest and most important client. For three years, starting from the 15th of September 2015, Guarding Professionals Ltd supplied SSGC with labour. Security guards were sent by my company to over 216 locations on behalf of SSGC.

My company specialised in the provision of labour, on an ad-hoc basis, in support of larger and well-established security companies across the UK. In doing this, my company sometimes worked with vetted service partners to fulfil our obligations. As standard practice, details of the guards were always supplied (guard name, SIA license number, and contact telephone numbers) to SSGC. Often SSGC would speak to and assess the suitability of the guards before deployment to its client's site.

The payment term of the agreement was thirty days after the invoice date. Initially, SSGC fulfilled this obligation without question. Sometime in 2016, the directors requested a meeting and pleaded with me to extend the payment terms to sixty days. A compromise of forty-five days was reached.

Despite this, SSGC sometimes did not fulfil its obligations and my accounts department often had to chase payment. Oftentimes, invoices took more than ninety days to be paid. Soon it became evident that SSGC was employing every trick in the book, to delay or avoid payment. They were very petty and could challenge five minutes of lateness and ask for a credit note before approving an invoice of twelve thousand Pounds (£12,000). It is difficult to believe, but even two Pounds can be a reason why a large invoice can be held up for weeks, if not months.

This got to a point where I told my accounts team not to challenge anything less than an hour. SSGC's account department was only operational Wednesday and Thursday 9 a.m. – 2 p.m. If you missed an opportunity to speak to a certain Frano who was in charge, you would have to wait for another week.

SSGC knew it was my company's biggest customer and the survival of my business depended on their patronage. Given the situation, I had to tread carefully. By November 2017, the business was suffering badly, and I decided that I needed to retrieve the debt and pay off the outstanding bills.

I, therefore, started chasing the outstanding invoices proactively. The total outstanding was just under ninety thousand Pounds (£90,000).

In December 2017, three thousand Pounds (£3000) was paid with a promise to pay October and November 2017 invoices in the first week of Jan 2018.

On the 12th of January, I received a rather bizarre email from one of the directors of SSGC asking for answers to the following questions, designed to trap or to lay down the basis and direction for the third battle. I have reproduced the email which set the wheels of the matter in motion:

Hi Richard,

Last week we discovered that one of our suppliers DPR Ltd had been sub - contracting some of our work. This in itself is not allowed without our express permission so is a contract breach, what has made this worse is the fact that the work was being farmed out to non ACS companies. Something that is not allowed by the SIA approved contractor rules at this point we also believe that there may be some PAYE offences. SSGC is an ethical company and will meet its obligation to investigate and report malpractice to the relevant authorities. We have taken the obvious steps of removing that company's approval to work as our supplier and are now contacting all of our suppliers to complete the following:

1. We want to inform you of DPR's methods so that you can take your own corrective action if they are a supplier to you.

2. Reaffirm that our contract does not allow for any subcontracting without authority, and we will not pay invoices that relate to sub-contracted works

3. We are taking the following investigative steps across our whole supply chain

4. Re read of all communications to 'scroll down' communication chains to ID other companies or named persons not directly contracted to SSGC

5. Direct contact with Security Officers to check their employer detail

6. PAYE (historic) staff payment records request from all suppliers

7. P file/application details for all staff used on SSGC contracts

8. We are adding to our supply chain management process

9. Random contact call to Security Officers working on SSGC to confirm

i. Employer details
ii. Hourly rate
iii. Last pay amount
iv. Confirmation that pay slips are used

10. Strengthening of our contract terms with regard to the use of subcontractors

11. Process for quarterly records check (PAYE & P File information)

Lorem ipsum

I would like you to consider the following options and let me know where you stand, please:

Option 1 – *You agree to the above and have not used subcontractor*

Action – invoices will be processed/paid as usual unless we find evidence to the contrary. If we do all invoices will be placed on hold and the approved status will be removed

Option 2 – *You agree to the above and have used subcontractors*

Action – Invoices relating to SC will be held and we will need a meeting to agree on a remedy (all others paid as usual). Your approval status with SSGC will not be affected as long as SC are ACS companies

Option 3 – *You do not agree with above*

Action – Work completed will still be investigated but invoice payment will not be affected unless Subcontracting is discovered. We will need to agree a wind down of your services over the next three months.

Can you let me know urgently what option fits please.

Kind Regards

After a careful read of the email, I concluded David was up to no good and that he wanted to bully me. I also noted that new conditions were introduced by SSGC into our working arrangements. I refused to answer any of the questions but demanded payment for the services rendered. In my response, I wrote the following.

Hi David,

Thank you for your email which I have just picked up and I wish to give the following initial response.

I note your comments about DPR which has nothing to do with our company, neither am I a party to the contract between SSGC and DPR. I can also understand the steps that you will want to take to safeguard your business, strengthen your contracts with your suppliers, and clean up your supply chain. These variations are purely within your remit.

On reading the content of your email, I conclude that you are neither privy to the contract between SSGC and Guarding Professionals Limited (GP) nor you have misconstrued the same. The contract between GP and SSGC is clear with no ambiguity at all, and we have consistently operated within its parameters. Indeed, your thought is at cross purposes with the spirit and letter of the agreement that has existed between the parties since September 2015. Even though I am entreating you to go back and read the said contract, I would like to point out to you that SSGC has consistently breached Clause 7.5 of the contract.

For the sake of convenience, I quote it here 'SSGC Ltd shall pay the contractor promptly, usually within 30 days end of the month upon receipt of a valid invoice, provided that SSGC Ltd is satisfied that the services for which the invoice relates have been performed fully in accordance with the Contract'

I shall also want you to read clauses 9.1, 9.5, 10.5.1 & 10.1.2 of the contract. These Clauses will speak to you, and you may conclude that you are in breach and pursuing a tactic that is completely unnecessary. Take notice that if we do not receive payment in the next 24 hours for October and November invoices which are both overdue in line with Clause 7.5 above, we will be left with no option but to instruct our solicitors to issue proceedings against SSGC to retrieve the money.

I shall however want to point out to you that any such variations should be discussed and agreed upon and must take only prospective and not retrospective effect. In the circumstance, I confirm that we are not considering any of the options as outlined in your email until you have remedied all your breaches under Clause 7.5. We are a responsible company, and our service delivery processes comply with all laid down laws and regulations. We are PAYE registered, VAT registered, ACS, ISO 9001, ISO 14001, and pay all staff accordingly. We work with some of the biggest security companies and have never had an issue with any of our clients.

Thank you.

The same day David Stubbs wrote to his co-director Antony.

Hi Antony,

Please see below with Richard. Are we behind on payments? Can you update me on the current position, please?

Kind Regards.

On the same date, his co-director Antony Monaghan wrote.

Hello David,

Richard is on an old contract that does state 30 days end of the month however we have never paid on those terms. As you know our customer demographic has moved to FM (and their 60-day terms) and we have moved all of our supplier payment terms to 60 days. Richard has always been amicable, we have never paid on 30 days, although I accept that we have not updated the contract. It's pretty clear from our historic payment cycle though that 60 days has been operated.

When we had a meeting, he stated he would like to continue to do business with us (as I gave him the option of managing down the account); I explained I can never meet 30 days as our clients are 60 – 90 days. My conversations and emails with Richard have all asserted a consistent position; SSGC working with GP to ensure payment for October & November needed to be in by the end of the month, his VAT point. We have had a mutual agreement that when I get stretched at my VAT point, we can delay payment as long as I ensure he gets his payment before his VAT point the following month.

I had agreed to ensure his October and November would be paid to ensure his real deadline was met. We agreed on this and he said he needed an early payment to get some cash flow in. I made a £3k payment on account in line with his request. I am working on his October and November being paid by the 31st of January to ensure cash is realised for his VAT cycle. This is the same as we agreed last quarter & can be validated through simple payment cycle analytics.

In summary, I believe we have an agreed position on payment, that I have paid the £3k as per Richard's request and that the Oct/Nov payment will be made on the 31st of Jan.

Best Regards

I challenged this, as I had agreed to forty-five days and not sixty terms of payment. In the meantime, David was aggressively demanding a response. When I threatened him with solicitors, he instructed his solicitors first. Heated exchanges between his solicitor and me ensued.

It had become clear that this dispute would drag on, although, at that time, I had no idea for how long.

The real battle was about to begin.

CHAPTER ELEVEN

CONFRONTING THE BULLY

On the 2nd of February 2018, I received a letter from SSGC's solicitors asking me to answer David's questions and stating that our invoices were on hold until all investigations were conducted.

The letter also threatened to report my company to the SIA for a breach of industry regulations. This was quite bizarre. The only reasonable conclusion any could draw was, 'We will not pay, and you cannot do anything.'

SSGC's solicitor made spurious, long-winded arguments and I was asked to provide PAYE details of all the staff, pay slips, and personal files for every security guard supplied to their client. The letter concluded by stating that failure to produce this would result in my company being reported to SIA. I knew that as the industry regulator, SIA would not hesitate to investigate a company if it received a report. The letter further stated that SSGC was in breach of its contract with its customers because of our alleged breach. Thus, SSGC would have to refund all the charges to its clients which were marked up by 32%. The sums were significantly higher than the overdue invoices we were claiming. I realised at this point that the SSGC was only trying to avoid payment and intimidate me.

After significant email exchanges, I concluded that I had to issue proceedings in court. As a starting point, I needed five thousand Pounds (£5,000) for court fees. Should I throw good money after bad? I asked myself. Litigation is risky and the outcome is unpredictable. I was aware of this. But the 'beast of a lawyer's instinct' in me said, go and get your money.

I had to engage a solicitor and barrister at considerable expense. I was of the view that as soon as the claim was issued, we would be able to settle, but I was wrong. SSGC had a plan, to intimidate, wear me down, and make me give up.

I spoke to a barrister friend of mine and engaged him on a 'direct access' basis. This was to save me solicitors' fees.

At this point, my company had run out of funds completely, so I spoke to Pastor Lawal, and he advised that I take a loan to keep the business afloat, while I pursued the matter in court. Pastor Lawal is very prayerful and said he would support me with prayers. He has stood by me in tough times, and I have always relied on his sage advice. He put me in contact with a consultant at a company called Funding Circles and within 72 hours I received forty-eight and a half thousand Pounds (£48,500). This money was vital. I was able to issue the claim and used the balance to pay some of my suppliers. In the meantime, I kept working hard, making sure the company won new business.

The claim was issued at the beginning of April 2018 and served on SSGC. It was a simple debt action and nothing else. I was surprised when SSGC issued a defence and counterclaim.

SSGC's defence was that my company was suspected of defrauding Her Majesty's Revenue and Customs (HMRC). It was alleged that work had been subcontracted to non-ACS (Approved Contractor Status) companies which was a breach of the SIA regulations and a breach of the agreement between us. SSGC therefore claimed not to owe my company and instead, it issued a counterclaim.

The counterclaim was just over one hundred and five thousand Pounds (£105,000). My barrister was out of the country at the time of service and missed filing a defence to the counterclaim, even though I had prompted him. SSGC's solicitor seized this opportunity and made an application for default judgment which was granted.

I had to engage the services of a solicitor at this point, to make an application to set aside the default judgement. Failure to set aside the judgment would mean SSGC would have been entitled to enforce the judgment. I was not impressed with my barrister's performance and had to change him.

The case took a new turn when SSGC's lawyers resorted to misusing a tool (Part 18 Request), in the Civil Procedures Rule (1998) to fish for information to bolster its defence.

A Part 18 Request is a formal request for a party to clarify or provide additional information about any matter which is in dispute in the proceedings. At least five such requests were made. The answers to the Part 18 Request were often used by SSGC to amend its statements of case, and so its position became rather fluid and evolving.

SSGC had a consultant called Guy whose witness statement was extraordinarily long but did not make much sense legally. Guy was directing how the case was to be run and was making noise for his money.

In the meantime, a certain Andrew from SSGC's operations team contacted all the one hundred and sixty security officers my company had supplied to them, to collect information that potentially could bolster their case or undermine ours. In Andrew's witness statement, he confirmed twenty-two of the one hundred and sixty officers had replied with varying degrees of information, which he used to prepare his witness statements.

David continued amending his witness statement anytime some new information was discovered either material or not. He was now using a tactic I call the 'scatter gun approach': Let us fire as many bullets as we can. We may be lucky. Though I did not have the financial resources, I had the resolve and determination to see the fight to an end. Yes, either in life or death, the end must come!

The excruciating thing was that I had to read hundreds of pages of these evolving documents and provide answers to my solicitor. It was really eating me up as I had a business to run. Costs escalated as I received fee notes from my barrister.

The amount of correspondence I had to deal with was overwhelming, but Kennedy Obierozie, my solicitor, started managing my emotions, temperament, and expectations. He knew I was breaking down.

It was in May 2019, when the court suggested we try mediation to settle the dispute. SSGC proposed I write off the debt and in return, they would offer me more work and a preferential charge rate. This made me angry.

I said, 'gone were the days when your forebears went to Africa, gave my forebears mirrors, and took gold away.' I turned to David and said, 'David look, I do not wash my face upwards, I wash it downwards.' This is a typical Ghanaian expression, which when translated literally means, 'I am not a fool.'

Guy resorted to the HMRC card. If we were not able to settle the matter, SSGC would have no option but to report it to HMRC.

'Go ahead and report me to HMRC,' I said.

By the end of July 2019, both my personal mobile telephone and the office line became unusually busy with calls coming from suppliers, employees, and the guards we supplied to SSGC. Everyone wanted to know why we were being investigated by HMRC. This was an exceedingly tough time. Some people sent copies of text messages they received from Andrew, encouraging them to provide information as they were working with HMRC to uncover tax fraud perpetrated by my company.

Even out of office hours, I had to pick up calls. I had to calm people down. I had occasions where some of my suppliers came to my office to demand payment. I saw a few videos online in which David granted interviews and made indirect references to my company.

I was reaching breaking point. My health was beginning to suffer. I could not sleep well, and my chest was always tense. I needed regular appointments with my GP and soon became a regular visitor to Accident and Emergency. My doctor asked me to take time off work.

'But this is no time to be absent from work,' I said to myself. I must be there, or else Guarding Professionals Ltd will collapse. After a while, my GP prescribed Sertraline (an anti-depressant) for me, which I took for nearly two years. No one is a Superman, at least not me. I needed this medication to keep me sane and alive to continue the fight.

On or around the 15th of September 2019, I received a call from the Fraud Investigation Service of HMRC. The person on the other side introduced herself and stated my company had been picked out to be investigated, as businesses engaged in the supply of labour were causing losses to HMRC. I was calm and waited for her to finish.

I asked, 'so when do you want to come for this investigation?'

She said she could not come before the end of October 2019. I knew I needed time to understand what was happening, the later the date of the investigation the better, I said to myself. So, we agreed on the 19th of December 2019.

It was clear that Guy had come good on his threat. I walked out of the office, not knowing where I was going, and needed some space to control my emotions. I walked around the business park where my office was located for about ten minutes before I could call my wife. She tried her best to calm me down.

Next, I called my accountant who said we should wait for the confirmation letter before taking any steps. Later that afternoon, I called my solicitor and asked to see him. We agreed that SSGC wanted to use any adverse finding from that investigation to bolster its defence. However, Mr Obierozie (solicitor) stated that I should not panic.

I checked the post every day for two weeks before the HMRC confirmation letter finally arrived. Though I was expecting it, the sight of the brown envelope sent my heart sinking into my stomach. I opened it and tried to read it. At first, I could not really understand the content. It was only on the third attempt that I started to comprehend the content.

The letter reads in part;

Fraud Investigation Services

HM Revenue and Customs

Dear Sir,

I am writing to confirm the appointment we made as detailed above. This is to discuss your VAT and PAYE records.

We are experiencing certain problems with businesses in your trade sector. These businesses include agency labour providers, contract cleaners, and security service providers. Fraud and general non-compliance with taxation rules and regulations is a major concern for the UK and there is a significant loss to the UK tax revenue. We are interested in all business dealings you, or any associated companies, may have relating to the provision of labour.

When we meet, I will need to see the following records, where they apply, for the period 03.16 to date. Please make sure that they are available for the visit.

Records needed at the visit

Annual accounts including profit and loss accounts

VAT account, showing the build-up of the figures that went on your VAT Returns

Bank Statements, cheques books and paying-in-books

Sales and purchase invoices

Cash books and petty cash book

Sales and purchase day books and ledgers

Factoring statements and contracts

'Record of takings

Payroll records, including time sheets and details of names addresses, and National Insurance numbers of all employees

General or nominal ledgers

Employment contracts

Customer Contracts

Any VAT working papers maintained by you or your accountant for you

Any relevant records.

I asked one of my colleagues to meet me outside. We sat in my car, and I gave him the letter to read. After reading it he looked into my face and said, 'going as far back as 2016?'

We both sat in the car for a while and I said, 'go back to the office, I need some quiet time to reflect on what this whole thing means.'

Questions raced through my head. After about thirty minutes I managed to call my wife. When she picked up, I said, 'the letter is here, and it is serious.'

'You have done nothing wrong, Kojo. We will go through it together,' she replied. I was on the phone with her for a long time.

As soon as I came off the phone, I called my accountant who said he had just arrived at Istanbul. He asked me to scan and send him a copy of the letter via email. He called me thirty minutes later and said, 'someone may have reported you, Richard'. I am away for 7 days and on my return, we will discuss this.'

Seven days was like an eternity.

The following day, I took the letter to my solicitor. After reading it, he said, 'the outcome of the investigation will either undermine your case or strengthen it. Either way, you have a good case.' I stayed in his office for the whole afternoon, finding solace in his presence.

That evening, I visited another friend of mine, Gabriel who is an accountant. He read the letter several times and said, 'we should pray.'

We prayed together. He encouraged me to be strong. He said the extent of documents and information HMRC wanted was not normal. According to him, the standard practice was for HMRC to go back for two quarters in one specific area of tax (PAYE, VAT, and if necessary, Corporation Tax). Going as far back as March 2016 for the two areas was extraordinary.

When my accountant returned from Turkey, we planned how to prepare for the investigation. To begin with, we would forensically re-audit all the financial records to see if we had missed anything. I was first tasked to collate all the bank statements, invoices and receivables, chequebooks, factoring statements, contracts, and paying books from April 2016 to November 2019 for this work to commence. Of course, alongside that, my normal day-to-day work to build back the business did not stop. I was working flat out and was incredibly stressed.

I developed sleeping difficulties and began relying on alcohol to help me catch a couple of hours of sleep each night. This, I very much regret. But it felt like the only way. The problem was that I would drink a few glasses of wine and go to bed at 11 p.m. By 2 a.m., I would wake up and start thinking, analysing, worrying, and going through the whole motion again.

I felt like everything was collapsing around me.

CHAPTER TWELVE

REDEMPTION

Whilst I was confident I had done nothing wrong, I was very apprehensive about the impending audit. These guys were coming from the Fraud Investigation Service. That was scary. Had I committed fraud unknowingly?

If anything was found, I knew my business would fold and my career as a lawyer would be over. It would affect my family, my kids, everything. All my dreams would die. Often, I would isolate myself and shed a few tears. But deep within me, I knew I had not done anything wrong, but the very thought of the investigators coming from the Fraud Investigating service was something I could not comprehend.

Meanwhile, SSGC kept coming up with new Part 18 Requests. Some of these questions were so complex that, deep thought had to go into answering them. I would usually have to speak to my solicitor before answering. The requests were simply a minefield.

By the first week of November 2019, I had to hire an independent accountant to help my regular accountant as we had so much to plough through. I was under immense pressure, but part of me said, 'Richard, you have one chance to fight for what is right.'

The principle of somebody trying to damage the other, because he does not want to pay a just debt, is wrong. You cannot run away from this fight Richard, I often said to myself. Fight until you have no strength to continue. I became so determined that I told my wife, 'Even if I die, make sure my estate continues the fight. Either in life or death, the case must continue to the end.'

When I got over-anxious, I would call Karl Davies, a particularly good friend of mine who would encourage me. He would say, 'Richard you are overthinking this problem. These guys are clowns, and they are playing a game'. He supported me to the end and at times when I was struggling to pay my bills, he would offer to lend me money. He was by my side, in good and bad times, helping me to open doors that turned my financial fortunes around.

I also sometimes called Paul West, an employee turned friend. I would vent my frustration, and he had the patience to listen and say positive words to encourage me. 'Take it slowly. You will have to live to see the end of this case. Stress will not help you.'

We attended the Pre Trial Review (PTR) on the 6th of December 2019. The purpose of PTR is to check if parties are trial-ready and have complied with all previous orders and directions. Looking at the bundles (all the papers from both sides) SSGC had filed five witness statements and an expert opinion – the opinion of Guy. This was noncompliant with the rules of the court.

My barrister made an oral application that Guy's expert opinion and the other witness statements should not be admitted into evidence. This was because, at the directions stage, SSGC had stated that it would only call one witness. If a party wanted to call more witnesses after the direction stage, the court must agree, and the other party must also be informed. This is because this can affect the time allocated for the trial and will also have cost implications.

However, SSGC's solicitors had sneaked in about five witness statements including that of Guy which stood as expert opinion. An expert evidence or opinion can only be relied on in court with the permission of the court or agreement of the parties, communicated to the court. SSGC had predicated its whole case or defence on Guy's expert opinion.

Guy's statement centred on the Private Security Industry Act 2001 and the UK's minefield of tax legislation. I know he did not understand the law. In fact, many seasoned lawyers will run away from UK tax laws anyway.

He misadvised his client and misled their solicitors as well. This was evident from all the statements from SSGC's witnesses. Because of the way my barrister made the application, SSGC's barrister was wrong-footed and could not really counter the argument advanced by my barrister. An order was therefore made not to admit Guy's expert opinion and the other witness statements. This means the foundation on which the defence was predicated was violently shaken. A small but very important victory.

The case was listed for two days, and a trial date was fixed for the 8th of January 2020. HHJ Saggerson (PTR Judge) in his order made it clear that this was a simple debt action and there was no need for expert opinion.

On the 10th of December 2020, I prayed with my wife before leaving the house and she suggested that if the accountants needed time to finish their work, before the investigation, I should call HMRC and rearrange the date. I said I was not prepared to do that.

I walked into the office the same day at 10 a.m. and the phone rang. It was HMRC saying they could no longer make the date of December 19th as one of their experts was unavailable. We agreed on a new date of 6th February 2020. Interesting, my wife turning into a prophet, I thought. Prophetess Joan, I joked when I called to tell her what HMRC just said.

Three days before Christmas, SSGC's solicitor made an application to the court to rely on expert evidence and asked the court to decide the application before trial. There was no reply from the court probably because of the Christmas festivities. On the 5th of January 2020, three days before the trial, SSGC solicitor contacted the court wanting the application to be determined as soon as possible or on the day of the trial. This was quite extraordinary. My legal team knew the reason. If Guy's opinion evidence or witness statement was not admitted, there was no defence.

On the 8th of January 2020 when we turned up for trial, the trial judge agreed to determine the application before the trial. To my bewilderment, the judge agreed that expert evidence would be helpful as the case was complex. So, the trial was aborted. SSGC's, barrister also made an oral application to call more witnesses. They initially wanted to call over twenty witnesses. The Judge felt that was not necessary and allowed seven to be called. When this order was made, I saw the joy on the face of Guy and David.

Whilst SSGC had all along argued Guarding Professionals was its subcontractor, I have always argued that Guarding Professionals was a labour supplier. Provision of labour and subcontracting are different things in the security industry. It is not just a label on a contract, but substance. The fact that subcontracting was attached to our agreement, does not mean the SSGC subcontracted work to Guarding Professionals. SSGC argued that I had never mentioned that Guarding Professionals was a labour supplier. The contract between the parties was written by SSGC and I expected them to understand what they had written.

This meant that 'subcontracting' and 'labour supply' had become the defining arguments in the case. The fact is that if Guarding Professionals was a subcontractor, it would have required permission from SSGC to use third parties or any of my service partners to supply the service.

Parties were also asked to appoint two joint experts, one with security industry background and the other with tax expertise. This was a hammer blow to me. The delay was causing me agony and money, while the determination of the case would most probably hinge on the expert's opinion. The search for experts commenced almost immediately.

The two accountants presented their reports to me on the 31st of January 2020. No errors were found as far as their audits were concerned. I had planned that if any errors were found, I was going to report that to HMRC before the investigation. My confidence level began to soar.

The morning of the 6th of February 2020 was chilly, when I set off from home to the office for the meeting with HMRC. Pastor Lawal called to pray with me and said, 'worry not because you have done nothing wrong.' Another friend of mine in Ghana, elder Michael K. Newton called to encourage me.

I had about six boxes full of every document imaginable. Just after 11 a.m. Joanne and Anthony from HMRC walked into the reception where I was waiting to meet them. I received them warmly and took them to the meeting room.

Joanne quickly started her questions and I answered each to the best of my abilities. Soon Anthony collected all the documents relating to PAYE. His first question came after about 45 minutes of ploughing through every detail. He looked at the timesheets, payslips, bank statements, and personnel files.

‘Who runs the payroll?’

‘I do,’ I answered.

‘Have you had any training?

I said, ‘Alan, my accountant, trained me.’

‘How do you keep up with changes in the legislation?’

I said, ‘we receive updates from HMRC, and my accountant often alerts me to changes that are taking effect.’

‘I have never seen a small company keeping their records so well,’ he said. ‘I have no further questions.’

Joanne, in the meantime, was ploughing through the bundle of files on her table and working her calculator vigorously. After about another thirty minutes, she started asking questions about my suppliers. Her final question was about a bill payable which did not have a VAT registration number. She asked if the company was VAT registered. Within a minute I had produced the VAT certificate of the company.

She shook her head and said, 'I have no further questions.' She addressed me briefly and stated that I should ask the supplier to state the VAT number on the invoice and concluded that if I did not hear anything from her within ten working days, I should consider the investigation over.

It was now my chance to speak. 'Will I receive a letter to confirm that the investigation was over and for that matter its outcome?'

'No,' she said, 'HMRC will not write such a letter.'

I told her about the litigation and SSGC's allegations and campaign of tax fraud against my company. Eventually, she agreed that she would have to speak to HMRC legal department. I called her at the end of February 2022 to find out whether the investigation had been closed.

She said, 'Oh yes Richard.'

I now demanded a letter to this effect as I had to demonstrate to SSGC that HMRC had come and gone with no adverse findings.

Reluctantly, she agreed and a week later I received a letter from HMRC stating that *an investigation was conducted,........* and no errors were found. That was the eureka moment. Upon the receipt of the letter, I cried. Maybe it was tears of joy. I was exhausted, but I kept going.

I scanned the letter and sent copies to my accountant and my solicitor. Moments later, I received a call from my solicitor 'Richard, your case is a lot stronger now. The final leg of your opponent's defence has crumbled', he said.

A copy was sent to SSGC. Their response was that they wanted to see all the documents I presented to HMRC. But there was no way I was going to open my house for my adversary. The potential tax liability was the cornerstone of the defence. This was already destroyed. Naturally, I felt SSGC needed to settle.

In May 2020, we made an offer to SSGC to settle for eighty thousand Pounds £80,000. It did not accept the offer, but as a strategy, we did not withdraw it.

Appointment of the experts and the issues to be opined upon amounted to separate litigation. After some four months, we managed to agree.

In July 2020, we received the reports of the experts, and lo and behold both reports vindicated my position. SSGC was obviously not happy and wrote to both experts, asking for clarifications. Both experts' positions remained the same in their replies. SSGC also proposed that the experts should come to court for cross-examination.

On the 5th of March 2021, we had another PTR before HHJ Boucher, which was adjourned five minutes before it started. Painful as it was, I needed to stay calm, and I did. Another PTR was scheduled for the 26th of August 2021 in which the trial date was set for the 13th – 17th June 2022. This was an agonising wait. Surprisingly during the intervening period, SSGC did not make much noise. Probably SSGC was tired or had played all its cards and was using the time to conduct 'self-introspection', I said.

On the morning of 25th May 2022, I received a call from my solicitor, and he said, 'are you sitting down? I have some news for you.'

My heart jumped.

'Your friends do not want to go to court. They want to settle,' he said.

For a moment I thought it was a prank, but he went further to state that they have offered seventy thousand Pounds (£70,000) and so he had asked them to put the offer in writing. Within twenty minutes I had an email from my solicitor which I now quote on the next page:

Without Prejudice Save as to Costs

Dear Kennedy,

Further to our call, I have discussed matters with my client in the run up to trial. Although its general position is unchanged, it is mindful of the litigation risk at trial. As a result, I am instructed to make an offer to your client to settle the claim and counterclaim with a payment to your client of £70,000. It is also a term that my client will pay your client's costs, to be assessed if not agreed.

As mentioned, my Counsel's brief fee will be incurred on Monday. As a result, if settlement is to be achieved, it will likely need to be before then and accordingly, I would be grateful if you could take instructions as soon as possible.

Kind Regards

Andrew

Later that afternoon, I had a conference call with my barrister and solicitor. We agreed that the offer was not good enough. I was clear that I would accept eighty thousand Pounds (£80,000) plus costs as a final settlement. The counteroffer of eighty thousand Pounds £80,000 was accepted the following day and the five days of gruelling trial was averted. At this point money was not my motivation, the victory of good over evil was what I enjoyed.

My business was doing very well and though eighty thousand Pounds (£80,000) is a lot of money, it was not going to change my financial position very much.

I had a little glass of wine that evening and played a lot of songs of praise. I walked through the emotions that evening with my wife. The following day I shared the good news with Karl, Pastor Lawal, Paul, my friends Mark, Ernest (OT), my nephew Albert, and all the others who stood by me during the fight. Not only did I win, but the truth had triumphed over evil.

In the intervening period, I became aware that several other companies had been treated in a similar manner by SSGC. The company had made a habit of this unethical behaviour. My company was the only one that has taken SSGC on successfully.

The costs involved in bringing the claim were about one hundred and twenty thousand Pounds (£120,000). SSGC's own costs would be well over this amount. Because SSGC had got away with this kind of behaviour many times, it was confident I would buckle down. I am happy I did not give up.

It was such a sweet victory.

In a twist of fate on Wednesday 9th December 2021, SSGC was among two hundred employers in the UK named and shamed by the government for failing to pay their lowest-paid staff the minimum wage. The employers were found to have failed to pay their workers one million, two hundred thousand Pounds (£1.2 million) in clear breach of the National Minimum Wage (NMW) law, leaving twelve thousand (12000) workers out of pocket, the publication stated.

SSGC continued this abysmal conduct when in case number 2501633/2021 heard at the Newcastle Upon Tyne Hearing Centre (hearing by CVP) on Friday 21st January 2022, a certain Mr F Yasi sued SSGC in the Employment Tribunal and won. His case was simple. SSGC failed to pay his accrued holidays.

In his judgment, Employment Judge Johnson wrote *'The Claimant's complaint of unauthorised deduction from wages (failure to pay accrued holidays pay) is well founded and succeeds. The respondent is ordered to pay the claimant the agreed sum of £363.10 in respect of accrued holiday pay. That is the net amount, and the respondent shall be responsible for the payment of any income tax and national insurance contribution thereon'.*

Employment Judge Johnson

Judgement Signed by Employment Judge On

1st February 2022.

I wonder why SSGC was taking the moral high ground when it was taking advantage of poor, vulnerable employees, and small companies.

In the Holy Bible, Mathew said in chapter 7: 4-5, How can you say to your brother, *'Let me take the speck out of your eye,' while there is still a beam in your own eye? You hypocrite! First, take the beam out of your own eye, and then you will see clearly to remove the speck from your brother's eye'.*

As Abraham Lincoln once said, 'You can fool some of the people all of the time and all of the people some of the time, but you cannot fool all of the people all of the time'.

I refused to be fooled. I refused to be intimidated. I refused to be worn out. I refused to be cowed. I renewed my energies and resolve when from afar I saw the crown and belt of justice.

Do not give up. Truth shall always prevail over evil. No matter how dark it becomes, daylight will surely come.

Remember, winners never quit, and quitters never win. The only way you can fail is when you stop trying.

CHAPTER THIRTEEN

A SENSE OF PURPOSE

All my life, I have had focus, direction, duty, and I suppose a sense of purpose. I have been driven forward as if striving to complete a mission. In the first instance, that meant academic and personal success, but secondly, and far more importantly, that meant providing for my family. I wanted to ensure that future generations did not have to grow up in the poverty I experienced as a child in my family.

It gives me huge satisfaction to know that this mission has largely been accomplished. The house I have built in Ghana is a wonderful home for my mother and siblings. The home I have in England, on the Essex coast, is one for my wife and children here. The things that I have achieved are a testament to the fact that hard work, perseverance, and determination pay.

Yet, I am not an extraordinary man. This is the point I want to make. I am a man who felt a sense of purpose and somehow kept sight of it, even when terrible events unfolded. The moral of the story is that if you keep hold of your dreams, they are always possible. Circumstances will crush you, never allow them to destroy you.

Of course, beyond that, I am greatly aware that life is not a mission or even a journey. It is an experience. In my early 50s, when this book was written, and with the goals I once set myself achieved, I have plenty of time to look back and maybe relax. But there is still much more I want to do, so much to achieve and something in me says 'keep going'.

But before then, I must face up to some long overdue internal work, and emotionally process the aftermath of my accident.

I have been through an ongoing issue with prosthetics, returning for annual appointments at the hospital where my accident happened. Sometime in 2021, I decided I needed to put that place behind me and change my appointment to a hospital in Essex, near where I live.

Over the years I have found that it is very difficult to find a prosthetic foot that fits well, at least in my case. Once you find one, you then need to get used to it. It is difficult to walk and often painful. My stump constantly changes shape because a kind of callous develops over time, which eventually peels off. So, it grows, then shrinks, grows, then shrinks. This means my prosthetic foot and the way my stump fits into my shoe need constant adjustment. It may not sound like a huge issue, but when you have to think about these things every time you take your shoes off or put them on, it consumes a lot of mental energy. Essentially, my injury is always on my mind. Always.

Strange, but the coping mechanism for losing my foot has been to keep busy. There are always things to, discuss, emails to send, and deals to make. But I can never forget my circumstance as it continues to cause me pain and inconvenience every minute of every day.

I remain so aware of how it has limited me. I cannot run and have been unable to play physical games with my children much as I want to. There are periods, especially in the evenings after work when all I can do is sit and rest. Despite my smiling, positive, businessman exterior, I can be bad tempered and needy. In those moments, I only survive on the love and consideration of those around me especially my wife and Harry my son.

My mother has still not actually seen the injury, even though I visit Ghana often; she knows about my accident, of course, but I have kept the reality hidden from her all these years. Maybe that is something I need to change. Or maybe it would be too much for her. I must think about that.

I have pondered, too, that perhaps one day I might undergo counselling. Even now, thoughts of 'why me?' occur to me. The randomness and sheer misfortune of what happened are not easy things to square in my mind.

One thing I know for sure, I would not have made it to where I am today without my three guardian angels, Mary, Mfon, and Diane. It is not possible to express in words how deep my gratitude is to them.

Their generosity, along with the actions of others, coupled with some good luck I had as I built my new life, rekindled my faith in God. I know I can never repay my indebtedness to the three guardian angels, but I have given away so much over the years in their honour. I shall continue to do so until I am here no more.

For a while, after my accident, I was bitter and angry and beset with self-pity. The kindness of others helped me emerge from that deep, dark tunnel and limp onwards into the light.

This is the most important thing because in Ghana, we have a saying:

'The bitter heart eats its owner.'
So, I am thankful with all my heart.

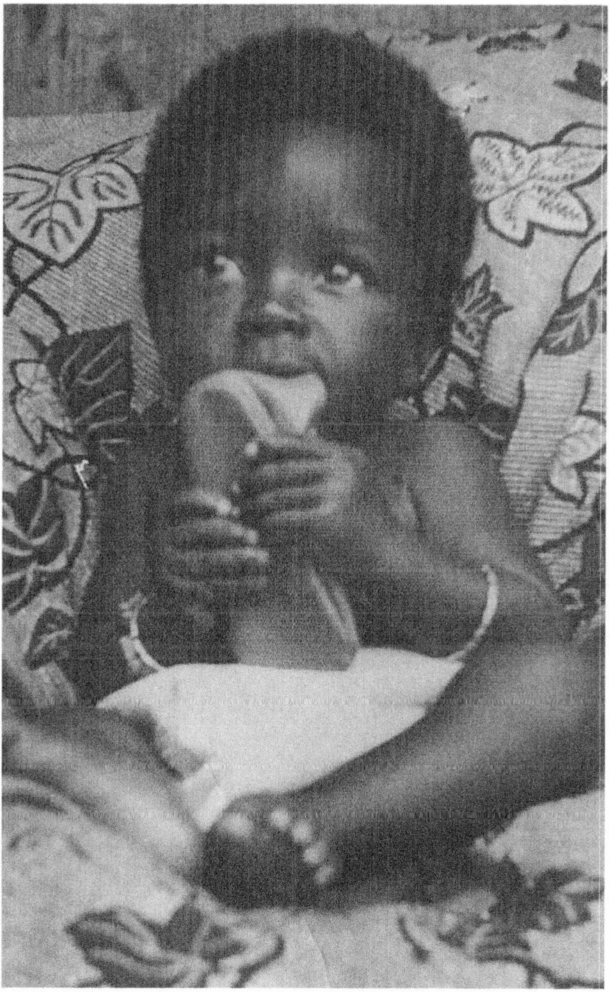

7 months old

Dreaming big
1995

Full of dreams
1996

My warrior Mum

This is where I was born.
Shared one room with my sibblings

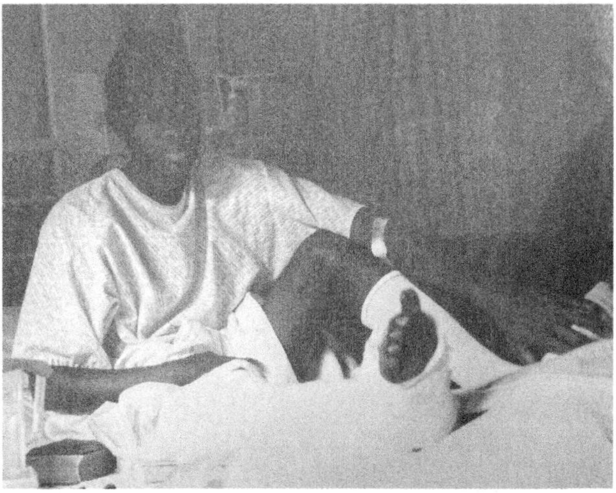

Losing hope and cursing God

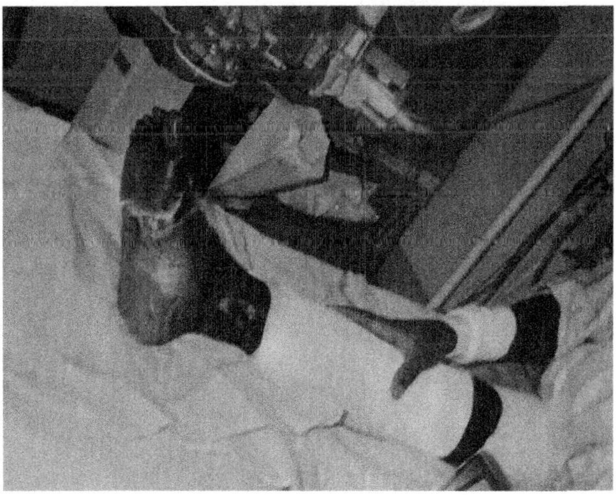

I cursed God even more

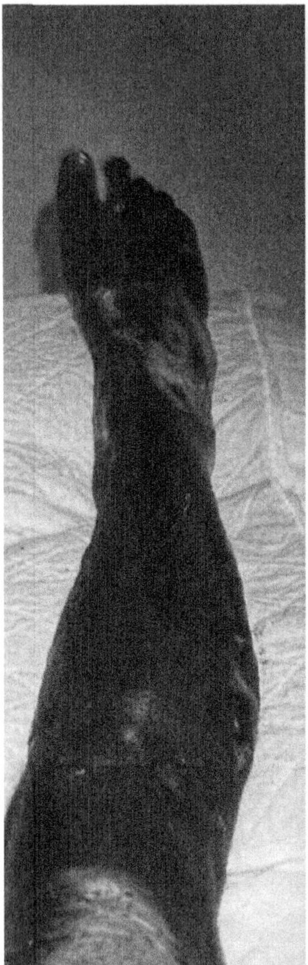

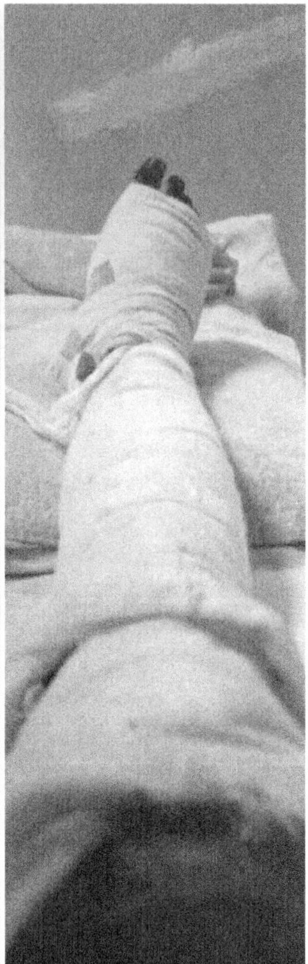

Desperate for a miracle *No End in Sight*

At a party

Entrance to my parents home

Inside the compound of my parents home

My wife and son

My three children

With guardian angel No 1 - Mary Hentall

With guardian angel No 2 - Diane Immelda Corbin Yearwood

30 Sept 2016
When called to the Ghana Bar

Guardian angel No 3
Mfon James

Fabulous

Called to the Ghana Bar

Proud Mama

At the Olympia London

ACKNOWLEDGMENT

I have been blessed to have had so many people who helped me every step of my life, without whom my story could never have been told.

I shall first like to thank God for his invisible hand in my life. When I look back, I see his mighty hands in everything I have achieved. He planted in my path three guardian angels - Mary Hental, Diane Corbin Imelda Yearwood, and Mfon James. I am grateful and cannot thank you enough. You gave me hope at the lowest point in my life and helped to change my life. Your kindness is legendary. May you continue to be a blessing to others.

Stand out thanks to my wonderful wife and friend, Joan Asare—the rock of my life. Your unwavering love, encouragement, and understanding have been instrumental in telling my story. My children—Jason, Annie-Lois, Harry, and Kai, I appreciate you. Not only are you part of the journey, but you gave Daddy the time and space to complete this work.

Special thanks also go to my mother Grace Aboegye and my father Godwin Acheampong, who despite all the odds, believed and instilled in me the virtues of hard work, integrity, and honesty.

I would also like to thank Pastor Godson Lawal and Dele Olawanle. Both of you in diverse ways mentored and showed me incredible love. You continue to inspire me.
I cannot forget to thank Karl Davies, Paul West, Ernest Osei Tutu, Mark Tsagli, Eric Tagoe, Kenneth Obieroze, and Albert Quansah. All of you in different ways stood by me in my most challenging times.

The list is endless, which leaves me so humbled, but to the very many others whose names have not been mentioned here, I am thankful for everything you have done in my life.

Finally, I will want to express my deepest appreciation to the readers of Crushed But Not Destroyed. I am sure in different ways you can relate to my story.

Thank you all from the bottom of my heart